History of India, From the First Euro]
Founding of the English East
William Wilson Hunter

Editor Introduction

The story of the preceding volumes was that of Medieval or Mohammedan India, the subject of this and the next volume comprises a new era in India's history – the opening-up of Hindustan to the West. Alexander the Great had found one of the routes in the early ages, but no Europeans, except the occasional traveller, the persistent trader from Roman days, and the devoted Christian missionary, had traversed this or the other pathways to India from Alexander's day until the time of the Moghul Empire.

The period of Mohammedan rule in India and the sway of the Ottoman power in the East had opened no new way for Occidental influence to enter Asia and had been prejudicial to any development of intercourse between Europe and India; but with the changes that were ushered in by the sixteenth century, the quest for India by the sea route began, and India was brought within reach of the maritime nations of Europe as a rich prize to strive for. The Portuguese, Spanish, Dutch, and English vied with each other in bitter rivalry to gain control of commerce and to establish a lasting supremacy in the East. The fullest and best account of this struggle will be found in the following pages from the late Sir William Hunter's pen.

Sir William Hunter's work, although comprising two bulky volumes in its fuller form, was not complete at his death, but in spite of that fact it will always remain one of the noblest monuments to his name. Through the courtesy of Lady Hunter and Sir William's original publishers, arrangements have been made to reproduce in this and the following volume of the present series that portion of his work which relates to the first European settlements in India down to the founding of the East India Company in 1600, and also the portion covering the earlier events of the history of British India in the seventeenth century. The permission thus graciously accorded is acknowledged here with appreciation. Sir William's text has been preserved practically without change, except for the omission of footnotes and for occasional modifications in certain matters of detail to agree with the rest of the series.

A new feature in the volume, however, is the Appendix which I have added, giving some early accounts by Mohammedan historians regarding the presence of Europeans in India during the Moghul Empire. I feel sure that certain of the descriptions and some of the expressions of opinion in this Appendix will be found to be interesting reading.

For particular assistance in illustrating this volume and the next by pictures from out-of-the-way sources I wish to thank Mr. George C. O. Haas, my student and ready helper, and I have had special aid from my friend, Dr. Justin E. Abbott, of Bombay, who has most kindly procured for the Grolier Society a special series of India photographs from which to select pertinent illustrations for the two volumes.

A. V. Williams Jackson

Author Preface

In this book I have endeavoured to complete a task which has occupied a large part of my life. Years ago my attention was drawn to the historical materials in the record rooms of Bengal, and the inquiries then commenced have been continued from the archives of England, Portugal, and Holland. I found that what had passed for Indian history dealt but little with the staple work done by the founders of British rule in the East, or with its effects on the native races. The vision of our Indian Empire as a marvel of destiny, scarcely wrought by human hands, faded away. Nor did the vacuum theory, of the inrush of the British power into an Asiatic void, correspond more closely with the facts.

Yet if we bring down England's work in India from the regions of wonder and hypothesis to the realm of reality, and if the Jonah's gourd growth of a night must give place for a time to the story of the Industrious Apprentice, enough of greatness remains. The popular presentment of the East India Company as a sovereign ruler, with vast provinces and tributary kingdoms under its command, obscures the most characteristic achievement of our nation in Asia. That achievement was no sudden triumph, but an indomitable endurance during a century and a half of frustration and defeat. As the English were to wield a power in the East greater than that of any other European people, so was their training for the task to be harder and more prolonged.

We have been too much accustomed to regard our Indian Empire as an isolated fact in the world's history. This view does injustice to the Continental nations, and in some degree explains the slight esteem in which they hold our narratives of Anglo-Asiatic rule. In one sense, indeed, England is the residuary legatee of an inheritance painfully amassed by Europe in Asia during the past four centuries. In that long labour, now one Christian nation, then another, came to the front. But their progress as a whole was continuous. It formed the sequel to the immemorial conflict between the East and the West, which dyed red the waves of Salamis and brought Zenobia a captive to Rome. During each successive period, the struggle reflected the spirit of the times: military and territorial in the ancient world; military and religious in the Middle Ages; military and mercantile in the new Europe which then awoke; developing into the military, commercial, and political combinations of the complex modern world.

This preliminary volume attempts a survey, rapid, yet so far as may be from primary sources, of the early phases of that conflict. After a glance at its commercial meaning to the peoples of antiquity, the scene opens with the Ottoman Power in possession of the Indo-European trade-routes. The first Act discloses the capture of the ocean highways of Asia by Portugal; an exploit which then seemed a maritime extension of the Crusades, and which turned the flank of Islam in its sixteenth-century grapple with Christendom. The swift audacity of the little hero-nation forms an epic, compared with which our own early labours in India are plain prose.

The second Act sets forth the contest of the Protestant sea-powers of Northern Europe with the Catholic sea-powers of the South for the position which Christendom had thus won in the East. Portugal, forced under the bigot rule of Philip II, was dragged into his wars with England and the Netherlands, and her fleets, which had grown up on the Asiatic trade, went to swell the wreck of the Armada. The task appointed to Elizabethan England stands out as a struggle not of Protestantism against Catholicism alone, but against Catholicism equipped by the wealth of both the West and the East Indies. Before Portugal could break loose from her sixty years' captivity to Spain her supremacy in the East had passed to the English and the Dutch.

Again the victors fought over the spoils. Those spoils lay chiefly not on the Indian coast, but in the Eastern Archipelago. India was then a half-way house for the richer traffic of the Spice Islands. The third Act unfolds the strife between the two Protestant sea-powers for this prize. The Netherlands had long contained the marts by which the produce of the East, trans-shipped at Lisbon to Bruges, Antwerp, and Amsterdam, was distributed to Northern and Central Europe. The capture of the Indian trade seemed to Holland a continuation of her just revolt against Portugal and Spain, a heritage from her hard subjection, and the seal of the independence which she had so dearly won. To England it was but the mercantile development, on an extended scale, of the sea enter-prise of the Elizabethan adventurers.

Holland brought to the struggle a slowly acquired knowledge of the Eastern trade, a vast patriotic subscription from the United Provinces, and a resolve alike of her people and her Government that the Spice Islands should pass to no hands but their own. England cared to risk only a small capital, split up into separate voyages and joint-stocks; for state sup-port she had but the quicksand diplomacy of the first James and Charles. The United Dutch Company was practically a national enterprise; the London Company was a private undertaking; and the fortitude of individual Englishmen in Asia availed little against the combined strength of Holland. The forces were too unequally matched, as will be seen when we come to describe the catastrophe which compelled the English to realize that, if they were to establish themselves in the East, it must be somewhere else than in the Spice Archipelago.

It may seem, perhaps, that I have allotted too much space to this threefold struggle – of Christendom against Islam, of the Protestant North against the Catholic South, and of the two Protestant sea-powers of the Atlantic – for the Asiatic trade. But a different law of proportion applies to Indian history, as I have conceived it, from that which sufficed for a melodrama of British triumphs. We must give up the idea of the rapid greatness of England in the East. In these chapters will be found, in part, the explanation of our unique position in India at the present day. Europe, just emerged from mediaeval-ism, was then making her first experiments in Asiatic rule. Medieval conceptions of conquest imposed themselves on her exploitation of the Eastern world; mediaeval types of commerce were perpetuated in the Indian trade. Portugal, Spain, and Holland established their power in Asia when these conceptions and types held sway. The English ascendency in India came later, and embodied the European ideals of the eighteenth century in place of the European ideals of the sixteenth. It was the product of modern as against semi-medieval Christendom. Yet even England found it difficult to shake off the traditions of the period with which this volume deals, the traditions of monopoly in the Indian trade and of Indian government for the personal profit of the rulers.

Characteristic features of our present Indian polity date from that early time. We shall see, for example, that the scheme of a European dominion in the East, built on native alliances and upheld by drilled native soldiers, was no invention of Dupleix improved upon by Clive. It developed with a slow continuous growth from the first Portuguese garrison in Malabar; through the Dutch system of subjugation by treaty; to the Feudatory States, the Sepoy army, and the Imperial Service Troops of British India. Much that we have accomplished our predecessors attempted, and not in vain.

Nor were their forms of home-control less fruitful of analogy than their experiments in Indian administration. The conquest and commerce of India were in Portugal royal prerogatives, almost a private estate of the Portuguese kings. The Dutch first tried separate voyages, then a United Company which became more and more national in character till it ended in a State Department. The English commerce with the East also started on the basis of royal prerogative – the prerogative of granting monopolies in trade. Under the later Stuarts the East India Company formed a battle-ground between the ancient privileges of the Crown and the growing strength of the nation; with the Revolution, the right of granting its charters passed finally to Parliament. Nor have the varied forms of organization which the Dutch devised for their Indian trade lacked counterparts in England; from the London Company's initial system of separate voyages, and its regulated or joint-stock associations of the seventeenth century, to the United East India Company and Board of Control in the eighteenth, and a Secretary of State for India at the present day.

But if resemblances between our, work in India and that of our predecessors are apparent, these chapters disclose differences more profound. The achievement of Portugal was the command of the ocean-routes, secured by settlements at strategic points along the shore. The Dutch dominion lay chiefly in the Eastern Archipelago. England's conquest was India itself. The native powers whom the early Portuguese encountered were petty coast rajas; the native powers whom the Dutch subdued were island chiefs. The English in India, schooled for a hundred years under the rod of the mighty Moghuls, brought a deeper experience and wider conceptions to a harder task. Their empire was to be not a few shore settlements like those of Portugal, nor an island dominion like that of the Dutch, but the Indian Continent. The question of territorial extension as against trade profits and sea-control arose with the first Portuguese viceroy in the East. It divided parties alike in the Dutch and in the English Companies; as, in its modern form of the Forward Policy, it still divides British opinion.

One fact stands clearly out. No European nation has won the supremacy of the East which did not make it a national concern; and no nation has maintained its power in the East which was not ready to defend it with its utmost resources. The prize fell successively to states small in area, but of a great heart – a heart beating with the throbs of independence newly won. We shall see that Vasco da Lama's voyage was but the last advance in an eighty years' march of discovery, commenced by the king who had secured the national existence of Portugal, and resolutely carried out by the successors of his house. The Dutch supremacy in the East formed the widest expression of their hard-earned freedom at home. It was the spirit which had hurled back Castile on the field of Aljubarrota that opened the Cape route to Portugal; and it was the spirit which had cut the dikes that gained the Spice Archipelago for Holland.

The question of questions, here and throughout, is not the size of a European nation, but what sacrifices it is willing to make for its position in the East. The united Spain and Portugal which lost the supremacy of the Asiatic routes formed a state on a much larger scale than the little Portugal that had won it. But to united Spain and Portugal, with vast armies to pay, the silver-yielding West Indies seemed a more profitable possession than the silver-absorbing East, and the resources which might have held the Asiatic seas were spent on the Catholic camps of Europe. In the first quarter of the seventeenth century, the strength of England was not less than that of Holland. But the English nation was as yet prepared to risk little for the Indian trade; the English sovereigns would risk nothing; the Dutch people and the Dutch Government were ready to risk much. In the middle of the eighteenth century the power of England was not greater than that of France, and France had servants in the East neither less brave, nor less skilful and fortunate, than our own. But the English in India had then their nation at their back; the French had not; and again the supremacy in the East passed to the people who were willing to endure most for it.

The crux in Asia has always been not the validity of rival titles, but which nation could enforce its claim. Nor has any Western nation preserved its ascendency in the East after it has lost its position in Europe.

The English connection with India has grown with the growth of England, till it now forms flesh of our flesh and bone of our bone. The Papal partition of the new Southern world between Spain and Portugal in 1493 forced England to try for a passage by the north; and her persistent quest for India and Cathay through the Arctic Circle in the sixteenth century became the starting-point of British exploration. At each stage our Eastern enterprise has taken the popular temper of the times. Garbed in religious phrases when England was Puritan, exuberantly loyal under the Restoration, a great constitutional question at the Revolution, cynical with the cynicism of the eighteenth century, yet quick to feel the philanthropic impulses of its close – those impulses which brought East Indian pro-consuls before the bar of an awakened public opinion, which were to give freedom to West Indian slaves, and to create a fresh field of national activity in Christian missions. A close monopoly as long as England believed in exclusive commerce, India now exhibits the extreme application of the English doctrine of free trade, and it forms the corner-stone of the new imperialism of Greater Britain.

These two volumes recount magnificent deeds done by Englishmen in Asia. Yet history cannot rank the generalship of Clive above that of Albuquerque, or the constructive genius of Warren Hastings above that of Jan Pieterszoon Coen. It is enough for a great man to be the express image of the greatness of his country in his time. The national spirit has been the dominant factor alike in our fortunes and in those of our rivals in the East. As the Cape route was discovered for Portugal before Da Gama hoisted sail in the Tagus, and as the Spice Archipelago would have passed to the Dutch without any tragedy of Amboyna, so Bengal must have become a British province although on some other field than Plassey, and the Mutiny would assuredly have been put down, even had no Lawrence stood in the gap in that great and terrible day of the Lord.

In this volume and the next there is presented a narrative of events in India's history since the country came into contact with the nations of modern Europe. In such a narrative the internal history of India, and its wondrous diversity of races, religions, and types of intellectual effort, forms not the least instructive chapters.

But the chief aim that has been kept in view is to trace the steps by which the ascendency of England was won in the East; the changes which it has wrought; and the measures by which it is maintained.

Chapter 1 – The Closing of the Old Trade Paths

To 1516 A.D.

On the establishment of the Ottoman Empire the medieval commerce between Europe and India was for a time blocked. That commerce started from the marts of Eastern Asia and reached the Mediterranean by three main routes. The northern tracks, by way of the Oxus and Caspian, converged on the Black Sea. The middle route lay through Syria to the Levant. The southern brought the products of India by sea to Egypt, whence they passed to Europe from the mouths of the Nile.

The struggle for these trade-routes forms a key to the policy and wars of many nations. When the Turks threw themselves across the ancient paths in the fifteenth century A.D., a great necessity arose in Christendom for searching out new lines of approach to India. From that quest the history of modern commerce dates. The prize for which the European Powers contended during the next three hundred years was a magnificent one. It had been grasped at by the monarchies of antiquity and by the republics of the Middle Ages. As they in turn secured it they had risen to their highest point of prosperity; as they in turn lost it their prosperity declined. The command of the Asiatic trade-routes was sometimes, indeed, the expression rather than the cause of the aggrandizement of a nation. But to the princes who fitted forth Columbus to seek for India in the West, and sent out Vasco da Gama to find it in the East, one thing seemed clear. The possession of the Asiatic trade had in memorable examples marked high-water in the history of empire; its loss had marked the ebb of the tide.

The most ancient of the three routes was the middle one through Syria. Ships from India crept along the Asiatic shore to the Persian Gulf and sold their costly freights in the marts of Chaldea or the lower Euphrates. The main caravan passed thence northward through Mesopotamia, edged round the wastes of Arabia Petraea, and struck west through the lesser desert to the oasis where, amid the Solitudo Palmyrena, the city of Tadmor eventually arose. Plunging again into the sands, the train of camels emerged at Damascus. There the Syrian trade-route parted into two main lines. The northern branched west to the ancient Tyre and Sidon and the medieval Acre and Ascalon. The other diverged southward by Rabbah, or Rabbath Ammon of the Old Testament, the Rabbatamana of Polybius, which is still locally known as Amman, and skirting the eastern frontier of Palestine passed through the land of Edom toward Egypt and the shores of the Red Sea. Its halting-places can still be traced. Thousands of Mussulmans travel yearly down the Barb-al-Hajj, or pilgrim way, by almost, although not exactly, the same route as that followed by the Indo-Syrian trade thirty centuries ago – no made road, but a track beaten hollow at places by the camels' tread.

The dawn of history discloses the Syrian trade-routes in the hands of Semitic races. The Chaldean or Babylonian merchants who bought up the Indian cargoes on the Persian Gulf, the half-nomad tribes who led the caravan from oasis to oasis around the margin of the central desert to Tyre or to the Nile, the Phoenician mariners who distributed the precious freights to the Mediterranean cities, were all of the Semitic type of mankind. The civilization of ancient Egypt created the first great demand for the embalming spices, dyes, and fine products of the East. But as early as the fall of Troy (1184? B.C.), if we may still connect a date with the Aeolic saga, Phoenician seamen had conveyed them northwards to Asia Minor and the Aegean Sea. Homer does not mention the name of India, but he was acquainted with the art-wares of Sidon, a Mediterranean outport of the Eastern trade. It was, however, in Egypt that the products of the Syrian caravan routes, and the possibly still earlier merchandise of Somaliland and the African littoral, found their chief market.

An emporium, perhaps originally a convict settlement from the Nile, sprang up at Rhinoculora, where the coast-line of Palestine adjoins Egypt. It probably received the traffic seawards from Tyre and by more than one land route through Palestine, and passed on the reunited volume of the Eastern trade to the neighbouring Nile valley. The Phoenician mariners of the Levant carried their alphabet, apparently derived from Egypt, to Greece and the countries around the Mediterranean Sea; the Sabwans of the Persian Gulf gave a cognate form of the same alphabet to India and the nations bordering on the Indian Ocean.

As the Phoenicians held the northern outports of the Syrian trade-route toward Europe, so the Edomites commanded its southern outlet toward Egypt. The Hebrews, also a Semitic race, occupied the country between the two, and the earliest traditions, not less than the verified history, of Israel, are intimately connected with Eastern commerce. The geography of Genesis is the geography of the Syrian trade-route; one of its most picturesque episodes, the sale of Joseph by his brethren, is an incident of the caravan journey. Abraham starts from the Chaldean, or Euphrates, end of the route near the Persian Gulf, and in four generations his descendants are settled at its south-western terminus on the Nile. The intermediate regions thus traversed formed the heritage promised to his seed, "from the river of Egypt unto the great river, the river Euphrates." This covenant is renewed in more precise terms in Deuteronomy, and grants to the Israelites the whole countries of the caravan route from the Euphrates on the east to the Mediterranean on the west, with Lebanon in Phoenicia as their northern, and the desert as their southern, boundary. The emporiums on the main branches of the Syrian route find mention in the Pentateuch, from Tyre, Sidon, and Damascus, down through Rabbah, Bozrah, and Edom toward the Egyptian and Red Sea end.

The political achievement of the Hebrew monarchy was to convert this promise, for a time, into a fact. The seventy-three years assigned to the reigns of David and Solomon saw both the process of conquest and its full commercial development. When David made Jerusalem his capital (about 1049 B.C., according to the generally accepted Biblical date), he found himself able from that stronghold to seize the positions which commanded the caravan route. On the north he occupied Damascus, the outlet of the desert track, and the key to the two branches of the Syrian trade westward to Tyre and southward to Egypt and the Red Sea. The King of Tyre sought friendly relations with him. David garrisoned Damascus together with the surrounding country, through which the spice caravans passed west to the Levant, and captured the great halting-place of Rabbah, about half-way down the eastern frontier route. His general, according to correct oasis strategy, had first secured the water-supply on which the town depended. David also completed the conquests begun by Saul among the Moabites and Edomites, who held the southern sections of the caravan track toward Egypt and the Red Sea. Before the close of his reign he made himself master of the entire trade-route from Damascus to Edom, controlled the country at both ends, seized the chief halting-place in the middle, and "cut off every male in Edom" toward the Red Sea and Egyptian outlets.

It was reserved for Solomon during his long rule of forty years, 1016–976 B.C., to put his father's con-quests to their mercantile uses. He strengthened his hold on the northern outlets of the trade by advancing into the desert and occupying the oasis of Palmyra. There he built or enlarged Tadmor in the wilderness, and thus gained command of the caravan track at a central point between the Euphrates and the Mediterranean. Tyre depended for her prosperity on obtaining a regular share of the Eastern trade by way of Palmyra and Damascus. The friendly intercourse of its king with David was therefore consolidated into a regular commercial treaty with Solomon; the Phoenician monarch supplying gold and the timber of the Lebanon hills in return for certain towns near the Tynan frontier, and for stated quantities of the agricultural produce of the Jordan valley. According to the Hebrew record, Solomon's sovereignty or overlordship extended to the Euphrates itself. Generally accepted maps show only the narrow strip between the Lebanon ranges and the Mediterranean, as belonging to Tyre, while the Jewish hinterland stretches in a solid block northeast to Mesopotamia. The promise to Abraham thus found its geographical fulfilment.

Having secured the northern outlet of the caravan trade toward Phoenicia, Solomon sought fresh developments for the Eastern trade at the southern extremity of the route. The Red Sea ends in two prongs, the Gulf of Suez on the Egyptian side, and the Gulf of Akaba on the Arabian, with the desert peninsula of Sinai jutting out between.

David's conquest of Edom not only secured the land-track into Egypt, but brought him to the Gulf of Akaba. Solomon occupied two harbours on its shores and launched vessels on its waters. Hiram, King of Tyre, supplied the materials and artisans for the construction of the ships, together with Phoenician sailors to navigate them, and built a fleet of his own on the same gulf. The two merchant navies sailed and traded in company, and poured the wealth of Ophir and the East into the new southern seaboard of Palestine.

This complete capture of the Syrian route forms the mercantile epic of Israel. The record of the rare and costly products with which it adorned Jerusalem, and of the transit duties which it yielded to the king, reads like a psalm rather than a trade catalogue. To some of those products, although bought up in the intermediate marts of the Euphrates valley, an Indian origin is plausibly ascribed – the ivory of which Solomon "made a great throne," his "precious stones," and "three hundred shields of beaten gold," the "traffic of the spice-merchants," the "apes and peacocks "of his pleasure gardens, and, probably, the sandalwood pillars "for the House of the Lord." From the Egyptian side the Hebrew king received linen yarn, horses, and a royal bride. The Song of Solomon, supposed by some commentators to celebrate his nuptials with Pharaoh's daughter, breathes the poetry of the caravan route, with its advancing clouds of dust, and its guards posted at night, every man "with his sword upon his thigh."

"Who is this that cometh out of the wilderness,

Like pillars of smoke?

Perfumed with myrrh and frankincense,

With all powders of the merchant."

The recollections of the Egypto-Syrian trade, its spices, pigments, and precious stones, survived in the Hebrew memory long after the possession of the route had passed from the nation. "Who is this that cometh from Edom with dyed garments from Bozrah?" wrote Isaiah in a dark period of his race. If the theocratic thesis of Jewish history sometimes obscures its political aspects, the national hatred against the cities which regained the Eastern trade after Jerusalem lost it, stands clearly out. Tyre is to be engulfed, or Made, in the words of Ezekiel, "a place for the spreading of nets in the midst of the sea." "The riches of Damascus" "shall be taken away"; "it shall be a ruinous heap." Rabbah, the ancient halting-place half-way down the southern caravan route, shall be "a stable for camels," "a desolate heap, and her daughters shall be burned with fire." "Bozrah shall become a desolation," a fire shall devour her palaces, and the heart of her mighty men shall be "as the heart of a woman in her pangs." The old rival Edom, toward the Egyptian terminus, forms the subject of a whole literature of denunciation.

Solomon's command of the Indo-Syrian route proved as evanescent as it had been brilliant. After his death (976 B.C.) his monarchy broke up. But the Twelve Tribes, even if they had held together, were a nation on too small a scale to maintain their independence against the mighty Powers which, during the next nine centuries, made Syria and Asia Minor their battlefield. Egypt from the south; Assyria, Babylonia, and Persia from the east; Macedonia from the north; Rome from the west – each sought to secure the countries that formed the outlets of the caravan routes. Whichever in turn was successful, the intermediate nationalities were crushed: the Jews among them. The reign of Solomon formed the climax alike of the territorial and of the mercantile ascendency of his race. I have dwelt on it for a moment, as it enables us to realize what the command of the Syrian caravan route meant to an ancient people.

It was a prosperity dangerous to the possessor. The coveted Syrian seaboard formed an Asiatic Palatinate forever shaking under the tramp of armies. In the seventh and sixth centuries B.C., Babylon was the entrepôt of the eastern routes, "the greatest commercial mart in the world." The Persian chastisements for her rebellions led to the transfer of her trade to Gerrha on the Arabian coast, and afterwards to Seleucia. In the time of Strabo, Babylon had dwindled to a village and an ancient name. By the conquest of Phoenicia and the Ionian colonies, Persia became a Mediterranean power, threatened the sea-commerce of Athens, and brought on the struggle between Greece and Asia fought out at Marathon, Salamis, and Platma. It was a Phoenician settlement, Carthage, that led to the great conflict between the rising maritime power of Italy and North Africa, represented by the Punic wars. The seizure of the countries along the Asiatic trade-routes by Pompey supplied the luxuries and splendours of Imperial Rome.

How complete was the Roman command of the regions through which that route passed is attested by ruins surviving to this day. Palmyra in the desert, respected by the earlier Roman emperors as an independent city, reached the height of prosperity under its prince Odenathus, who received from Gallienus the title of Augustus, and was acknowledged as a colleague in the Empire. Bostra in the Bashan country, four days' journey south of Damascus, became under Trajan the beautified capital of the Roman province of Arabia, and the headquarters of the Third Legion. As a trade emporium before its capture by the Arabs it had won the title of "the market-place of Syria, Irak, and Hejaz." The spacious Roman amphitheatre at Rabbah, midway down the south-eastern trade-route, may still be traced.

Photographs shown to me by a recent traveller along the track disclose at many places the enduring work of Rome, from the straight road whose solid pavement slabs emerge above the sand, to fluted columns, sculptured temples, and public buildings half-buried beneath it.

The Saracen Arabs who, under the conquering impulse of Islam, next seized the countries of the Indo-Syrian route (632–651 A.D.), soon realized its value. They were a trading not less than a fighting race, and Bassorah and Baghdad under the caliphs became the opulent headquarters of the Indian trade. An Arabic manuscript in the British Museum narrates an embassy of a Byzantine emperor in the tenth century A.D. to Baghdad, which recalls the visit of the Queen of Sheba to Solomon in the tenth century before Christ. The same splendid profusion was displayed by the Caliph as by Solomon to his guest; the products and art-work of India were alike conspicuous at the Arab and the Hebrew capital. The Caliph's curtains were of brocade with elephants and lions embroidered in gold. Four elephants caparisoned in peacock silk stood at the palace gate, "and on the back of each were eight men of Sind." If Baghdad was, from the commercial point of view, the more spacious Jerusalem of the caliphate, Bassorah was its Alexandria on the Persian Gulf, which received from the East, and passed on to the West, "the wealth of Ormus and of Ind."

The Crusades blocked for a time the Syrian route. But the Crusades, although impelled forward by the religious fervour of northern Europe, were speedily organized for trade purposes by the Mediterranean Republics. The fleets of Venice, Genoa, and Pisa victualled the armies of the Cross, accompanied their progress along the Syrian coast, and divided their spoils. Under the Christian kingdom of Jerusalem (1099–1291) the Syrian caravan route revived. It exchanged the products of the tropical East and of the North for the hard cash of the Crusaders, and a regular fur market existed in Jerusalem for the sale of ermine, marten, beaver, and other Siberian or Russian skins. In 1204 the capture of Constantinople by the Crusaders, with the Earl of Flanders raised' to the Imperial dignity, promised to medieval Italy a restoration of the affluence which had flowed from the East to ancient Rome.

But new forces were upheaving in further Asia, destined to overthrow Saracen. culture and Christian trade with a common ruin. About 1038 A.D. the Seljuk Turks had burst upon Persia. Two centuries later the gathered strength of the Mongols poured over Asia under Chingiz Iaan (1206), ravaged through Poland under his son, and under his grandson wrested back Russia to barbarism. In 1258 Baghdad went down before the Mongol hordes, and the Saracenic caliphate was shattered. The tidal wave of devastation spread over the countries of the Syrian caravan track, at times leaping forward in irresistible masses, then pausing to gather volume for the next onrush. In 1403 Timur drove the Knights Hospitallers forth from Smyrna to their island stronghold at Rhodes. By that time the Mongols and Turks had partially blocked the middle trade-route from the Persian Gulf to the Mediterranean, and were preparing to seize the northern trade-route by way of the Black Sea.

The main northern route started from the Indus valley and crossed the western offshoots of the Himalayas and the Afghan ranges to the Oxus. On that great river of Central Asia the products of India were joined by the silks of China, conveyed from the western province of the Celestial Empire by a caravan journey of eighty to a hundred days. The united volume of traffic struggled onward to the Black Sea, due west by the Caspian, southward by Trebizond, northward by the Volga and the Don, as shown on my map. A route referred to somewhat obscurely by Strabo, but with a new interest in our days, seems to have crossed the southern basin of the Caspian. The galleys proceeded up the twelve-mouthed Cyrus River, the modern Kura, as far as its channel allowed.

Their cargoes were then transported by a four or five days' land journey over the water-parting which separates the Caspian from the Black Sea, until they reached the point where the river Phasis became navigable. Its stream carried the precious freights down to the emporium of the same name at its mouth on the Black Sea: a Milesian settlement whence the pheasant is said to have been brought to Europe by the Argonauts – the legendary pioneers of that branch of Eastern trade. The Russian railway from Baku on the Caspian to Batum on the Black Sea, with Tiflis as the meeting mart midway, corresponds to this ancient route up the river valleys and across the watershed.

Besides the Oxus routes ending on the Black Sea, other roads led from the Indus valley to the west.

After crossing the Hindu Kush the southern tracks touched the capitals of Bactria, Parthia, and Media, eventually reaching Baghdad, Palmyra, Tyre, and Antioch. The spoil found by the soldiers of Heraclius in the palace of King Khosru Parviz shows how the products of India had entered into the courtly life of Persia in the seventh century A.D.

The difficulties of the Central Asia routes to the Black Sea, with their deadly camel journey of alternate snows and torrid wastes, rendered them available only for articles of small bulk. They never attained the importance to India which the two southern trade-routes, by the Syrian caravan track and by the sea-passage to Egypt, acquired. They formed, however, ancient paths between Europe and China, and received prominence from the blocking of the Syrian route in mediaeval times.

From the Black Sea the products of the East went chiefly to Constantinople, but they also penetrated into Europe by the Danube and other channels. The trade appears to have helped toward the early civilization of the Crimea and the Danubian provinces. The emporium of Theodosia on the Crimean coast was, like Phasis, originally a trading colony of the Milesians. It survived, although in decay, to the time of Arrian, and reappears in a variant of its modern name, Kaffa, under the Greek emperor who sent the embassy to Baghdad in 917 A.D.

The Eastern trade by the Black Sea long formed a source of wealth to the Byzantine empire. Conflicts between Christian and Saracen in Syria enhanced its importance, and the Venetian merchants who settled at Constantinople when captured by the Crusaders in 1204, further developed the route. During the fifty-eight years of the Latin empire at Constantinople (1204–1261) the Venetians engrossed the Eastern commerce by way of the Black Sea. Venice stretched her armed trading stations, practically in unbroken succession, from the Adriatic to the Bosphorus, and stood forth before the world as the acknowledged Queen of the Mediterranean.

On the re-establishment of the Byzantine empire (1261), the Genoese, whose mercantile jealousy of Venice overcame their orthodox faith and led them to assist the Greek emperor in the expulsion of their Catholic trade-rivals, took the place of the Venetians at Constantinople.

They received the Pera quarter, commanded the harbour, planted fortified factories – or trading-posts under the superintendence of a factor as head – along the European and Asiatic coasts of the Euxine, occupied part of the Crimea, and made its old emporium at Kaffa the headquarters of the Eastern trade by the Black Sea route. About 1263 they rebuilt the ruined city of Kaffa. Its spacious harbour, with deep water and firm anchorage for a hundred ships, played a leading part in the Genoese monopoly of the Euxine.

Of scarcely less importance was Soldaia, also on the southeast coast of the Crimea. Its Greek settlers had long acted as middlemen between the Asiatic and Russian traders, and, strengthened by a Venetian factory, they grew rich on the Indian commerce by the Black Sea route during the thirteenth century. Marco Polo the elder owned a house at Soldaia which he bequeathed in 1280 to the Franciscan friars of that port. In 1323 Pope John XXII complained that the Christians had been driven forth by the Mongols from Soldaia, and "their churches turned into mosques." Yet Ibn Batuta (1304–1377) still reckoned it as one of the five great ports of the world. In 1365 Soldaia became a fortified factory of the Genoese, who traded there till the downfall of the Byzantine empire, and whose defensive works survive to this day.

These ports on the Crimea formed the inlets of the Eastern trade to the Russian emporium of Novgorod. The position of Novgorod gave it access by the Dnieper to the Black Sea on the south, and by the Neva to the Hanse towns of the Baltic. In its marts the spices and fabrics of the East were exchanged for the furs of the North, and distributed to Western Europe. "As far back as the eleventh century," writes Consul Perry, "Gothland's commerce with the East by way of Novgorod was already of much importance." The marshes and lake region around Novgorod defended it for a time against the Mongol hordes. Its merchants carried not only the art-work but also the currency of Asia to Scandinavia; and twenty thousand Cufic coins minted in about seventy towns of the Abbasid caliphs are said to have been at one time preserved in Stockholm.

The tide of wealth which thus set toward Venice and Genoa from the Black Sea procured for them a period of splendour scarcely less striking than that of the Saracen, or of the briefer Jewish, ascendency over the Indo-Syrian route. Trebizond, at the south-eastern extremity of the Black Sea, had grown into the terminus and emporium of a great Asiatic trade-route by way of Erzeroum. But the Turks pressed ever closer on the outskirts of the Byzantine empire. The bitter trade hatreds of the Genoese and the Venetians rendered a continuous coalition impossible for the Mediterranean Christian powers. Each aimed at engrossing the Eastern commerce, and each would gladly have seen its rival ruined.

For a time indeed it appeared as if the lands and riches of the Byzantine emperors were to be divided by an unholy connivance among Serbians, Albanians, Genoese, and Turks. In 1444, Genoese vessels ferried an army of forty thousand Ottomans across the Bosphorus, at a ducat a head, to do battle against the champions of Christendom. Nine years later, in 1453, the Turks finally took Constantinople. In 1475 Kaffa fell to their all-devouring armies. The Genoese colony with its warehouse palaces at Pera, its trading strongholds along the narrow seas, and its two factories in the Crimea, went down in the wreck of the Byzantine empire.

By the middle of the fifteenth century, therefore, the Mongol and the Ottoman hordes had blocked both the Black Sea and the Syrian routes of the Indo-European trade. The third, or southern maritime, route to Egypt claimed perhaps a less ancient origin; it was destined to survive the other two in medieval times, and again to become the highway of Eastern commerce in our own day. Herodotus narrates the naval expedition of Sesostris, the Egyptian monarch of the fourteenth (?) century B.C., from the Red Sea along the Asiatic coast, and his conquest of the intervening countries between the Persian Gulf and the Mediterranean. This would suffice, apart from any legendary invasion of India proper, to give to Egypt for a time the command of the Syrian caravan route. The Father of History mentions that he had himself seen the sculptured memorials of the conqueror in Syria and Asia Minor – a statement seemingly verified by their modern discovery on the roads to Smyrna and to Beirut. Nor is it needful to examine too closely the evidence for the Sesostris Canal from the Nile to the Gulf of Suez, or its identity with the similar works on which later Egyptian kings, Necho, Darius son of Hystaspes, and Ptolemy Philadelphus, laboured.

The northerly winds that blow down the Egyptian side of the Red Sea during most of the year rendered the navigation up its western shores difficult for vessels of the Old World. Indeed, the perils of the coasting trade from the emporiums of Indian commerce on the Persian Gulf to the Red Sea seem to be commemorated by names along its route – by the Cape of the Indian's Grave on the southeast of Arabia, and by the Straits of Bab-al-Mandab, or Gate of Tears, at its south-western extremity. The author of the "Periplus" (about 80 A.D. 7) gives a chapter to the "dreadful coast" of Arabia, without harbours, and peopled by tribes who had no mercy for shipwrecked crews.

Under the enterprising Egyptian King Psammetichus, however (671–617 B.C.), Carian and Ionian settlements at the mouth of the Nile had opened out the Mediterranean to the Indo-Egyptian trade – a trade which that monarch further secured by Syrian and Phoenician wars, if we may judge from Herodotus. Alexander the Great perceived the capabilities of the Nile delta as the natural entrepôt for the East and West. Alexandria, which he ordered to be built on the neck of land between Lake Mareotis and the Mediterranean, grew into the emporium of the Eastern traffic for the Greek and Roman world, eclipsed the ancient glories of Tyre, and, on its modern site, again became one of the strategic positions of the globe as the half-way house of Indo-European commerce.

From the founding of Alexandria (332 B.C.) its Asiatic trade grew with the improvements in the sea-passage. At a very early period the Arab navigators tried to avoid the northerly winds which sweep down the Egyptian coast, by unlading their cargoes near the modern Kosair, and transporting them overland to Thebes, the capital of the Nile Valley – the fame of whose twenty thousand war-chariots and hundred gates had reached the ears of Homer. Ptolemy Philadelphus did much during his long reign (285–247 B.C.) to concentrate the Eastern trade at Alexandria, the new capital of Lower Egypt. He reopened the ancient cutting from Bubastis to the Bitter Lakes, and was only stayed from completing his canal to the Gulf of Suez by fears lest the Red Sea would flow in and submerge the delta.

To escape the difficult navigation of the Suez Gulf, Ptolemy Philadelphus founded, on the headland near its mouth, Myos Hormos (274 B.C.), whence the Indian wares were carried across the desert to the Nile Valley. To avoid still further the northerly head winds on the passage up the African coast, Ptolemy created the emporium of Berenice at the southern extremity of Egypt on the Red Sea, and honoured it by his mother's name, Berenice, which this trading centre is said to have transmitted through the Italian form verenice to modern commerce in the word varnish. A caravan journey of 285 Roman miles conveyed the eastern freights through wastes and mountains to Coptos on the Nile, with regular halting stations along the track. Some of these still dot the desert, and the proposed Assuan–Berenice railway, for which a survey has been made, would revive the old trade path from Ptolemy's harbour to the Nile Valley by a shorter cut. Railway communication seems destined, indeed, to reopen the ancient paths of Indo-European commerce. The Russian line to Bokhara represents, not too exactly, an old route from China by way of the Oxus; the long-projected Euphrates Valley Railway would be the modern counterpart of the Syrian caravan track.

The final development of the Indo-Egyptian route did not take place until three centuries after Ptolemy Philadelphus, when the pilot Hippalus discovered the monsoons, or more strictly speaking, worked out the regular passage by means of them (circ. 47 A.D.). These periodical winds blow from Africa to India for about six months, and from India to Africa during the other six. While, moreover, the Egyptian coast-passage is impeded by northerly winds during most of the year in the upper part of the Red Sea, the navigation at its southern end is aided by regular variations in the air currents, southerly winds predominating from October to June, and northerly winds from June to October. The establishment of the emporium at Berenice in the third century B.C. thus paved the way for a vast expansion of the Eastern trade as soon as the monsoons were put to their mercantile uses.

Egyptian merchant fleets sailed from Berenice or Myos Hormos in July, rounded the modern Aden with a halt at Kane in August, and were blown rudely across the Arabian Sea to Malabar by the middle of September – a voyage of sixty or seventy days from the Egyptian to the Indian coast. Having sold their western freights and bartered their bullion for eastern cargoes, they started from India at the end of December, and were wafted more gently back by the winter monsoon to their Red Sea harbours about the beginning of March.

This monsoon route became the chief channel for the bulkier produce, as well as for the precious gems and wares, of India; enriched the ports along its line; and made Alexandria the commercial metropolis of the Roman Empire. Pliny lamented the vast shipments of gold and silver sent from Europe to pay for the products of Asia. "In no year," he says, "does India drain our Empire of less than fifty-five millions of sesterces (£458,000), giving back her own wares in exchange, which are sold at one hundred times their prime cost."

Of this great commerce, while Egypt still remained a Roman prefecture, two accounts by actual traders exist. "The Circumnavigation of the Indian Ocean" describes it within a hundred years after the discovery of the monsoon winds by the pilot Hippalus. Written probably by a Greek merchant who had settled at the southern Red Sea emporium of Berenice and voyaged to the East, its composition is assigned to a date between 80 and 161 A.D. It gives the seaports on the route, specifies as many as ninety-five of the chief articles of traffic, and forms a wonderfully complete presentment of the state of Indo-Egyptian trade in the first century of our era.

"The Christian Topography of the Universe," by Cosmas Indicopleustes (circ. 535–547 A.D.), takes up the story about four hundred years later. Its author, a merchant and apparently also a navigator, had become a monk of Alexandria in later life, and wrote out in his cell the recollections of his voyage. To these he adds much cosmical speculation, "not built on his own opinions or conjectures," he assures us, "but drawn from Holy Scripture and from the mouth of that divine man and great master, Patricius." Apart from such mystical physics, he gives an account of the trade of Malabar and the Eastern Archipelago, with topographical details and notices of Indian products, in some respects fuller and more exact than can be found in the Arab geographers of the next seven centuries. In his time Ceylon had become famous as the meeting-place of the merchants of the East and West; of the galleys from Egypt and the Persian Gulf, with the heavier junks of China. Cosmas not only mentions China for the first time by name as Tzinista (cf. Chinistan), a designation which admits of no dispute, but he had also a fair idea of its position, lying to the northeast of Ceylon as the Euphrates delta lies to the northwest, and with the same circumambient ocean as the highway to both.

Prom this time, China plays a distinctive part in the Indo-European trade. Three ancient land routes have been traced from India to China; Indian colonies settled on the Malacca coast and in the Eastern Archipelago; Indian missionaries spread their Buddhist faith from Central Asia to Burma, Ceylon, and Cathay. At the Red Sea, or western extremity of the route, Indian sailors seem to have given a Sanskrit name (apparently Dwipa-Sukhadhara, or Island Abode of Bliss) to the island of Socotra, as they did to Sumatra (presumably a variant of Sanskrit Samudra, Ocean) half-way along the ocean course. At the eastern extremity the very ancient Tao coinage, or "Knife-Cash" of China, has been ascribed to sea traders from the Indian Ocean, who before 670 B.C. marked their bronze knives with distinctive symbols so as to convert them into a returnable currency.

It must be remembered that during ten centuries (250 B.C. to about 700 A. D) Buddhism was the dominant political religion in India, and that it was a religion of enterprise both mercantile and missionary by land and by sea. We are told that Indian 'merchants were found in Alexandria, although the supposed statue of the river deity Indus in that city was probably the gift of a Greek. A Chinese book of botany, ascribed to a prefect of Canton in the fourth century A.D., mentions plants then growing in Canton, which seem to have been brought by traders from Arabia or the Roman provinces. The trading colony of Arabs at Canton, dating from the times when they still followed Sabean rites, included at the beginning of the seventh century A.D. an uncle of Mohammed. Hearing of his nephew's fame as one sent by God, the worthy merchant returned to Arabia only to find the prophet dead. "Has he left any message for me?" he asked. "None," was the reply. "Then I shall go back to China. If the prophet had other views for me, he would have left me word." He accordingly sailed again for Canton, where his mausoleum is shown. But the early connection of China with India and the West has hardly yet emerged from the twilight of tradition.

The learned Chinese scholar Edkins has examined the influence of Arabian or Babylonian trade-inter-course on the science and geographical conceptions of ancient China. Of that influence he finds evidence under the Chow dynasty in the history of Chinese astrology, metrology, and astronomical instruments. The pre-Alexandrian astronomy of India also had probably a Chaldean origin. It was a commercial dispute that brought about the first Mussulman conquest of an Indian province. In 711 Mohammad ibn Kasim led a naval expedition against Sind to claim damages for the ill-treatment of Arab merchantmen and pilgrims near the mouth of the Indus on their voyage from Ceylon.

During the following centuries the Indian Ocean became an outlying domain of Islam. The Arab geographers mapped the course from the Persian Gulf to China into "seven seas," each having a name of its own, and with the Arab-Chinese harbour of Gampu on their eastern limit. As the Chinese trade grew in volume, Ceylon had to share her gains as the meeting mart of Europe and Asia with entrepôts still further east. Abulfeda, the princely geographer of the fourteenth century (1273–1331), mentions Malacca as the most important trading-place between Arabia and China, the common resort of Moslems, Persians, Hindus, and Chinese.

While Greek and Roman merchants had enriched themselves by the Indo-Egyptian trade, the actual sea-passage from India to Egypt, like the actual caravan route from the Persian Gulf to the Levant, remained in the hands of Semitic races. Colonies of Arabs and Jews settled in an early century of our era, or perhaps before it, on the southern Bombay coast, where their descendants form distinct communities at the present day. The voyages of Sinbad the Sailor are a popular romance of the Indian trade under the caliphs of Baghdad, probably in the ninth century A.D. Although inserted in the "Thousand and One Nights," they form a distinct work in Arabic. Sinbad traverses the ocean regions from the Persian Gulf to Malabar, the Maldive Islands, Ceylon, and apparently as far as the Malay Peninsula.

A series of Arabian geographers and travellers bring down the narrative to the fourteenth century. Egypt had passed to the Saracens in 640 A.D.

But under its Fatimite caliphs and later Mamluk sultans, the Indo-Egyptian trade continued to flourish, and probably gained rather than lost by the temporary interruption of the Syrian land route during the Crusades. Ibn Batuta (1304–1377), who travelled for twenty-four years in Asia, Africa, and the Mediterranean, declared Cairo to be the greatest city in the world "out of China," and mentions Alexandria as one of the five chief ports which he had seen. Two other of them were on the Bombay coast, and all the five (namely, Alexandria in Egypt, Soldaia or Sudak in the Crimea, Koulam or Quilon and Calicut in India, and Zaitun or Chincheu in China) were fed by the Indian or Chinese trade.

But the same Turkish avalanche that had thrown itself across the Syrian and Black Sea routes was also to descend on Egypt. The Venetians on their expulsion from Constantinople in 1261 transferred their Eastern commerce to Alexandria, and after the capture of Constantinople by the Turks in 1453, Egypt for a time enjoyed almost a monopoly of the Indian trade. The monsoon passage was in fact the one channel that remained always open from India amid the Mongol and Turkish convulsions along the caravan routes. The growth of the Ottoman navy from 1470 onwards began, however, to imperil the Mediterranean outlets of the Indo-Egyptian trade. It was in vain that Venice in 1454 made an un-Christian peace with the Moslem conquerors of Constantinople, and sought to secure the passage from the Adriatic to Alexandria by fortified stations and island strongholds along the route. Venice had ruined the naval power of Genoa, and the gallant defence of the Knights Hospitallers at Rhodes in 1480 could only delay, not avert, the Ottoman seizure of the Mediterranean highway.

In 1470 the Turks wrested the Negropont from Venice with a fleet of one hundred galleys and two hundred transports. Before ten years passed their squadrons swept the Adriatic and ravaged along the Italian coast. In their work of destruction the Turks were aided by an even more savage sea-force from the West. The rise of the Barbary corsairs is usually treated as an episode of medieval piracy. As a political factor, it formed the maritime complement of the Turkish con-quests by land. While the Mussulmans held southern Spain., treaties between the Mohammedan and Christian princes tried to restrain the buccaneering ports for which the inlets on the African coast seemed made by nature. But on the overthrow of the Moorish power in Spain by Ferdinand and Isabella in 1492, the scourge of African piracy was let loose on the Mediterranean. The reign of terror reached its height under the great corsair admirals after 1504. Yet during a quarter of a century before this final development, the galleys of the African Moors outflanked the Venetian and Genoese fleets in the western Mediterranean, and thus strengthened the Turks in their struggle for the naval supremacy in the Levant.

The same year, 1480, that saw the temporary failure of the Ottomans at Rhodes saw also their capture of Otranto in Italy. In 1499 they crushed the naval force of Venice at Zonchio and Lepanto. By this time the Sea of Marmora and the Black Sea had become Turkish lakes. Turkish fleets and fortresses dominated the Hellespont, the Syrian coast, the Greek harbours, and most of the island trading-stations of the Aegean and the Levant. The rise of the Ottomans as a sea power thus blockaded the Mediterranean outlets of the Indo-Egyptian trade as their rise as a land power had obstructed the Indo-Syrian and Black Sea routes. Their seizure of Egypt in 1516–1517 was merely the finishing stroke of the conquests by which, in the preceding century, the command of the old Indo-European highways had passed to the Turkish hordes.

While a great necessity thus arose among the Christian nations to search out new trade-routes to India, we must not exaggerate the extent to which the old ones were closed. Alike in the Euphrates valley, in Syria, and in Egypt the Ottomans ousted Semitic dynasties of a comparatively civilized type. For a time, also, they trampled down the refinements in which those dynasties delighted. But the rude despoilers grew themselves into luxurious potentates, and although their Mongol nature was incapable of the higher Semitic culture, it took on a veneer. The period of avalanche passed; the need of the Indian trade-routes for exits toward Europe remained as insistent as before.

Nor were the Turks indifferent to the taxes and transit duties that could be squeezed from the traffickers whom they despised. The Asiatic commerce, whether by Syria or by Egypt, often interrupted and at times blocked, was never altogether destroyed. Genoa and Venice still distributed their Eastern wares, in an impeded flow, to the European nations. After the fall of Constantinople to the Turks in 1453, and the partial blockade of the Nile by the growing Ottoman navy, Famagusta in Cyprus became the Venetian headquarters of the trade in succession to Alexandria after 1475. It did business with Egypt under the Mamluk Sultans until 1516, and resumed its intercourse when the Nile valley settled down, after that year, beneath Ottoman rule. For nearly a century Famagusta remained a leading emporium of the Levant, until itself taken by the Turks in 1570–1571.

The Ottoman seizure or obstruction of the Indian trade-routes brought disaster not alone to the Mediterranean republics. The blow fell first on Genoa and Venice, but it sent a shock through the whole system of European commerce. The chief channel by which the products of Asia reached the central and northern nations of Christendom was the Hanseatic League. This Hanse, or "Association" of towns and merchant colonies for mutual defence, had developed in the thirteenth and fourteenth centuries into the great trade organization of northern and central Europe. At the beginning of the fifteenth, its settlements stretched from Russia to the Thames; appeals from distant Novgorod were heard by its chief tribunal at Lübeck; Augsburg became the central depot of Europe, and her banker-weavers, the Fuggers and Velsers, rivalled the merchant-princes of Venice and Genoa. Bruges, the north-western depot of the Hanseatic trade, had at one time representatives of twenty foreign courts in the warehouse mansions which lined her canals. "There are hundreds of women here," the wife of Philip the Fair of France is said to have exclaimed when she visited Bruges at the beginning of the fourteenth century, "who have more the air of queens than myself."

The Indian trade formed an important contributory to this Hanseatic commerce. When the Eastern traffic began to dry up, its European emporiums declined; when, as we shall see, the Cape route was substituted, they withered away. "Grass grew," says Motley, "in the fair and pleasant streets of Bruges, and seaweed clustered about the marble halls of Venice." Augsburg, which had financed the commerce of central Europe, dwindled into a provincial town. Novgorod suffered in addition to mercantile decay the abolition of its charters by Ivan III in 1475, and the carrying into captivity of a thousand of its richest families. Its later sack by Ivan the Terrible has left little besides a fortress and cathedral, rich in relics, to bear witness to its ancient greatness. The Mediterranean marts of Eastern commerce, from Lisbon looking out on the Atlantic, to Venice once mistress of the Adriatic and the Levant, shared in varying degrees the common fate. In the first years of the sixteenth century the Indo-European trade of the Middle Ages lay strangled in the grip of the Turks.

Chapter 2 – The Quest for India by Sea

1418–1499

The European nations had not stood idle spectators of this collapse of their medieval Eastern commerce. At first indeed the dim masses in Central Asia appeared to Christian princes as possible allies in their struggle for the Holy Places against the nearer Saracens. In 1245 Pope Clement rv sent a Franciscan agent to the Tartars in Persia, and two years after-wards another friar to the Tartar camp on the Volga. St. Louis during his ill-fated crusade (1248–1254) found the Tartar hordes advancing on the common enemy from the East. The casual concurrence seemed to prom-ise an identity of interest, and envoys passed between the Tartar chief in Persia and the French king. About the same time St. Louis despatched William de Rubruquis, a Minorite friar, to the Tartar Khan on the Black Sea (1253).

Rubruquis's narrative formed the delight of medieval students, Roger Bacon among them; and its veracity is attested by modern geographical research. At first passed to the learned world in manuscript, it has been repeatedly printed in whole or in part. But it failed to enlighten Christian diplomacy as to the true character of the forces at work in Western Asia. Rubruquis visited various Tartar chiefs from the Black Sea to the edge of the great Mongolian desert, and returned by the Volga and the Caucasus, much impressed by the Tartar power. The Turkish kingdom in Asia Minor struck him as of no treasure, few warriors, and many enemies. Two ambassadors from Castile had seen the Turks shattered by Timur in the carnage at Angora in 1402, and were honourably entertained by the Mongol conqueror. The Black Sea route obtained a delusive prominence, and the menacing strength of the Turks continued for a time obscure to Catholic Europe;

It was by this Black Sea route that the Venetian family of merchant travellers, the Polos, originally started toward India and China in 1260. The imperishable record of the greatest of that name, Marco, is the masterpiece of travel in the Middle Ages, and has been illustrated by the patience and learning of a foremost geographer of our day. Marco Polo reached China by land and returned by the long sea passage, via the Straits of Malacca, Malabar, and Persia, after an absence of twenty-four years (1271–1295). His work gives the first account of India by a Christian writer since that of Indicopleustes in the sixth century A.D. But the mercantile enterprise of Venetian and Genoese traders, like the missionary zeal of the friars who preceded and followed them, proved power-less to keep open the Black Sea route when the Turks threw themselves across the path. A similar fate befell the attempts of Christian land-explorers by way of Syria and Egypt. Yet the list of such European travellers during the fourteenth and fifteenth centuries, including the remarkable journey of the Russian Nikitin (1468–1474), bears witness to the persistence which they brought to the task. Two of the great land-travellers overlap the discovery of the Cape route. One of the last of them, Ludovico di Varthema, found the Portuguese struggling for a settlement in India, was present at their sea-fight with the Zamorin in 1506, and took service under Portugal as a factor in Cochin on the coast of Malabar.

The achievement that rescued the Indian trade from the thrall of the Infidel, more effectively than combined Christendom had ever delivered the sacred places of Palestine, was the work of a nation which even then ranked among the small ones of Europe. But, with the exception of the imposing figurehead of the Holy Roman Empire, the contrast between the leading and the lesser States at the beginning of the fifteenth century was by no means so marked as it is now. The modern first-class Powers, France, Germany, Austria, Russia, Italy, Great Britain, were not yet built up. Spain was still divided between Castile, Aragon, and the Moors. Europe remained a continent of principalities, duchies, counties, little oligarchies, and little republics.

The Mediterranean States that had engrossed the Indian trade during the Middle Ages were cities rather than countries. The new Power destined to supersede them was essentially a nation, a nation still aflame with the patriotism that had won its independence, and cherishing an undying hatred against the Moors whom it had driven forth.

In the thirteenth century Portugal attained its European limits At the end of the fourteenth it entered on a career of splendour under a singularly able and long-lived line of kings. John I, or the Great, of the house of Aviz, and his four successors ruled from 1385 to 1521, and raised their country from an outlying strip on the Atlantic to the ocean outpost of Christendom.

Their combined reigns form the heroic age of Portugal. That period commenced with a firm affiance with England; it ended with the complete establishment of the Portuguese in India. It is marked throughout by a fierce hostility to the Mussulmans, and by a spirit of exploration which in Portugal succeeded to and absorbed the spirit of the Crusades.

The English alliance formed the keystone of the policy of John the Great. The friendship of Portugal and England had, indeed, been of slow and solid growth. Toward the close of the twelfth century a body of London crusaders halted on their way to the Holy Land to help the Portuguese against the Moors. The end of the thirteenth and beginning of the fourteenth centuries found King Diniz "the Labourer" in close correspondence with our Edwards I and II. In the middle of the fourteenth century a marriage was negotiated, although not carried out, between Edward the Black Prince, of England, and the daughter of Affonso IV of Portugal. In 1352 Edward III issued a royal proclamation commanding his subjects thenceforth and for ever to do no harm to the Portuguese; the next year a commercial compact was entered into and signed in the city of London; and on May 9, 1386, the Treaty of Windsor united the two countries by a close affiance.

The claims of John of Gaunt, Duke of Lancaster and son of Edward III, to the throne of Castile for his Spanish wife, brought about a still nearer connection with Portugal. The Portuguese king discerned in those claims a source of support in his hereditary struggle with the Castilian dynasty. It seemed, indeed, as if the States of western Europe naturally ranged themselves into a league of England, Portugal, and Flanders against France, Scotland, and Castile. In 1385, five hundred English archers under three squires of John of Gaunt fought on the decisive field of Aljubarrota which secured the independence of Portugal against Castile and placed the house of Aviz, with John I as its head, on the Portuguese throne.

In July, 1386, a couple of months after the Treaty of Windsor, John of Gaunt himself landed at Corunna with his Castilian princess, two daughters, 180 galleys, two thousand lances, and three thousand of the famous English archers.

One daughter he promptly married to John the Great of Portugal (February 2, 1387); the other daughter, by his Spanish wife, to the Prince of the Asturias, heir to the throne of Castile. He himself renounced his Castilian claims, and imposed on his two sons-in-law a truce which lasted till 1411.

Philippa, daughter of this masterful Englishman, "time-honoured Lancaster," was worthy to be the consort of a great king and the mother of heroes. The friendship of England, which her marriage with John I cemented, proved a tower of strength to her husband during his epoch-making reign of forty-eight years (1385–1433). In 1398 a body of English archers came to his aid, and in 1400 he was created a Knight of the Garter – the first foreign sovereign who received that honour. In 1415 our Henry V sent provisions and troops to join the Portuguese expedition against the Ceuta Moors, and again in 1428 a force of English lances heard King

John of Portugal's battle-cry. That battle-cry was one dear to English men-at-arms, "Saint George!" and as a Knight of the Garter John bore the dragon for his crest. The recumbent statue of his English queen, Philippa, at Batalha shows the face of a beautiful woman, with finely cut features, a lofty forehead, and a look of firm sense. Simple and religious in her habits, carrying abstinence so far as to under-mine her health, her chief pleasure in life was to make peace between enemies, and her great occupation to educate her children. "To do good was with her a necessity of existence."

Of the eight children whom this noble and devout Englishwoman bore to John I of Portugal, the eldest survivor (called Duarte after his great-grandfather, our Edward III) succeeded to the Portuguese throne. Another son, Pedro, became famous as the royal land-traveller of his century; a third, Fernando, won by his chivalrous self-sacrifice and patient sufferings in Moorish captivity the title of The Constant Prince.

But the most illustrious of them was her fifth child, born on Ash Wednesday, March 4, 1394, and imperishably known in history as Prince Henry the Navigator. On coming of age in 1415 he won his spurs at the Portuguese siege of Ceuta, the Mussulman stronghold of north-western Africa just within the Straits of Gibraltar. His splendid gallantry at the gate, where he stemmed, for a time alone, the rush of the Moors, and his calm intrepidity as a leader, gained the plaudits of Christendom. His biographer states that the Pope, the Emperor of Germany, and the Kings of Castile and of England each invited the young hero to take command of armies.

The capture of Ceuta and its political consequences awakened a different ambition in Prince Henry's breast. Its conquest had converted a chief emporium of the Moors into a bulwark of Christendom against them. But Ceuta drew the sources of its wealth – its gold-dust, ivory, and tropical products – from the interior and the coast districts of west Africa. How to reach these provinces of Nigritia by sea and thus cut off the wealth of Morocco at its source, became the daydream of the young prince. His zeal for the aggrandizement of Portugal was combined with a passion for maritime exploration and an ardour to extend the dominions of the Cross. The first question which he set before him was whether the north-western coast of Africa should belong to Mohammed or to Christ. Portuguese chroniclers date his exploring expeditions as far back as his eighteenth year, 1412. But from a Bull of Pope Nicholas V it seems likely that he definitely commenced this work after his exploit at Ceuta (1415), when he had just attained manhood. In 1418, while still only twenty-four, he made his Great Renunciation and, turning his back upon the world, retired to the wind-swept promontory of Sagres at the southern extremity of Portugal.

On that barren spur of rocks and shifting sands and stunted juniper, with the roar of the ocean forever in his ears, and the wide Atlantic before him inviting discovery from sunrise to sunset, he spent his remaining forty-two years, a man of one high aim, without wife or child. Amid its solitudes he built the first observatory in Portugal, established a naval arsenal, and founded a school for navigation, marine mathematics, and chart-making. Thither he invited the most skilful pilots and scientific sailors of Christendom, from Bruges near the North Sea to Genoa and Venice on the Mediterranean. Thence, too, he sent forth at brief intervals exploring expeditions into the unknown South: expeditions often unfruitful, sometimes calamitous, even denounced as folly and waste, but which won the African coast as an outlying empire for Portugal.

He died at Cape St. Vincent in 1460, having expended his own fortune together with his splendid revenues as Grand Master of the military Order of Christ on the task, and pledged his credit for loans which he left as a debt of honour to his nation. His tomb, in the same beautiful chapel where his English mother rests at Batalha, bears by the side of his own. arms as a royal prince of Portugal, the motto and device of the Garter conferred on him by our Henry VI, and the cross of the Portuguese Order of Christ. On the frieze, entwined with evergreen oak, runs the motto which he solemnly adopted in young manhood – Talent de bien faire – the resolve to do greatly.

The king, wrote Diogo Gomez, "together with all his people mourned greatly over the death of so great a prince, when they considered all the expeditions which he had set on foot" – in the words of his monument on the gateway of Fort Sagres – "to lay open the regions of West Africa across the sea, hitherto not traversed by man, that thence a passage might be made round Africa to the most distant parts of the East."

The maps of the two preceding centuries, and especially the Laurentian portulan, or chart, of 1351, together with notices by the Christian and Arabic geographers of the same period, enable us to understand exactly what Prince Henry achieved. A tradition, for which the Revival of Learning was destined to supply a historical basis, came down through the dark ages that ships had sailed round Africa in very ancient times. The three years' voyage from the Red Sea to the Mediterranean, sent forth by Pharaoh Necho (617–601 B.C.), seemed discredited to Herodotus on the ground that now forms its best evidence of authenticity. For who could then believe the mariners' tale that the sun which rose on their left hand during one part of their voyage rose on their right during the remainder?

So little impression did the voyage make on the minds of sober men that Eratosthenes found no record of it in the Alexandrian library in the third century before Christ, nor Marinus of Tyre in the second A.D. Hanno's shorter expedition down the western coast of Africa (circ. 570 B.C.) had the good fortune to be inscribed on a temple at Carthage, and passed thence into the geography of the Greek and Roman world. A century later (circ. 470 B.C.), according to Herodotus, a nephew of Darius undertook to circumnavigate Africa in commutation of a sentence of death by impalement, returned unsuccessful, and was executed by Xerxes.

The legend of these expeditions, like those of the Insulae Fortunatae and Homer's blissful realms of utmost earth, waxed faint in the centuries of eclipse which followed the overthrow of Roman civilization. Even to a friend of Ovid the Atlantic was a sea of darkness. Two schools of geographers had arisen, one affirming the Atlantic to be a great lake with no outlet into other seas, the other maintaining the possibility of circumnavigating Africa. An Alexandrian philosopher of the seventh century A.D. thus sums up the opinion of his time: "Certain men have supposed, following a foolish tradition, that the Atlantic is united on the south with the Indian Ocean. They pretend that several navigators have been carried by accident from the Atlantic Sea to that ocean, which is evidently false. For it would require that the ocean should extend quite across Libya, and even under the torrid zone. Now it is impossible for men to navigate there on account of the burning heat that prevails."

The Venetian map of Marino Sanuto (circ. 1306) embodies the same idea and describes a great tract as uninhabitable by reason of the heat. Even the light of the Moslem geographers grew dim. Ibn Khaldun, himself an African and well acquainted with the facts of African navigation just before Prince Henry's expeditions, describes the Atlantic as "a green or black ocean into which ships do not venture far, for if they get out of sight of land they rarely find their way back."

Yet the legend of a passage round Africa to India lived. The Laurentian or Medicean map of 1351, although based on conjecture and vague tradition beyond the Gulf of Guinea, shows the trend of that gulf to the eastwards, and a continuous passage round to the Red Sea. But Cape Non, about eight degrees down the African coast from Gibraltar, was reckoned, according to the Portuguese proverb, the safe limit of navigation in medieval times, and continued to be so when Prince Henry commenced his explorations. Further south the promontory of Bojador, emphatically "the headland," stretched into the ocean and shut out the Sea of Darkness beyond it from the European world. Two Genoese galleys sailed in 1291 A.D. toward those latitudes "that they might go by sea to the ports of India," but never returned. Indeed, so barren of results, had been the ancient Carthaginian expedition down the African coast, that only one example of passing Cape Bojador, and that a chance flotsam of shipwrecked Arabs, can be admitted between the voyage of Hanno in 570 B.C. and the fifteenth century after Christ.

To round Cape Bojador and open a path through the Sea of Darkness to the Indian Ocean – to the thesauris Arabum et divitiis Indiae – was the purpose of Prince Henry's life. It mattered not that unsuccessful voyages brought on him the reproaches of the Portuguese nobles. The patient prince realized that Cape Bojador was not to be passed by a leap, and set himself to explore gradually down the African coast. It was thus that he won his title as "The Originator of continuous modern discovery," and proved what one great man backed by a race of sailors can achieve, in spite of the doubts of science and the discouragement of grandees.

Neither in the islands of the Atlantic nor on the coast of Africa was he first in the field. Certain of the Azores had been reached by Portuguese ships steered by Genoese pilots at the beginning of the fourteenth century and appear in the Laurentian map of 1351. Two runaway lovers from England are said to have been blown south by a storm to Madeira in 1344 and to have perished there. The Portuguese expedition to the Canaries in 1341 has been told by Boccaccio from the letters of Florentine merchants at Seville. But these voyages yielded little or no result. It was re-served for Prince Henry deliberately to rediscover what had formerly been found, and to make discovery go hand in hand with commerce and colonization.

The same remark applies to the African coast. Beginning with the discovery, or rediscovery, of Porto Santo and Madeira in 1418–1420, the prince steadily pushed his expeditions southward until in 1434–1435 his captains rounded Cape Bojador in latitude 26°, and opened up the Sea of Darkness beyond it to Christian ken. After that achievement further progress was only a question of time. Certain dates may however be noted. Between 1441 and 1444 his squadrons explored the African coast to Cape Blanco and Arguin Bay; in 1447 they reached the Rio Grande within twelve degrees of the equator – where "the north star appeared to them very low." By 1455–1456 they had fairly established intercourse with the natives along the shores of Senegambia. Before 1460 his captains had laid open the Cape Verde Islands to the Portuguese, and in that year Prince Henry died.

To understand the part played by India in the later history of Portugal, and the patriotic sentiment with which the Portuguese still cling to their Indian possessions, we must realize the efforts which the discovery cost the nation and the slow steps by which it was achieved. The forty-two years of Prince Henry's explorations (1418–1460) added only eighteen degrees of latitude to the verified geography of the north-western African coast, from Cape Bojador to Sierra Leone, or not four days' course of a steamship in our times. He barely penetrated the edge of the vast Sea of Darkness.

This small result from so much toil and devotion was due in part to the poor sailing qualities of his vessels, in part to the imperfections of his nautical instruments and to the rudimentary state of navigating science. The fleets of the Mediterranean had largely consisted of galleys propelled by slaves. But oars could ill contend with the mighty waves of the Atlantic, nor was it possible to provide food for hundreds of rowers on the long voyages which Prince Henry planned. His first problem was to develop the oared galley or weak sailing craft of an inland sea into the ocean-going ship, and to supersede the thews of men with hungry mouths by the winds which ate nothing. The question of sails versus oars dates from the earliest period of navigation, and has been discussed by the latest naval historians. Prince Henry required not only a new type of vessel but also a new adaptation of an old force to propel it. It was the Atlantic as against the Mediterranean, and the sailing ship as against the slave-rowed galley.

In this task, as in his actual discoveries, Prince Henry had predecessors. Contemporary drawings disclose the transition from the medieval galley, a sort of beaked barge with upper structures for fighting men and the lower deck crammed with rowers, to the heavy galleon and galleasse, and the handier caravel with its lateen rig. The caravel marks an early stage of the development of square into side sails which added much to the tacking power of ships, and enabled them to put the wind to its full use on ocean voyages. Prince Henry adopted the caravel as his model for distant explorations and developed its navigating qualities. Cadamosto, although a Venetian, declared that the Portuguese caravels – craft of fifty tons increasing in the sixteenth century to two hundred – were the best sailing ships afloat.

The rudeness of the nautical instruments and of the nautical science of the time was a hindrance to Prince Henry scarcely less serious than the imperfections in the rig and build of his ships. The magnetic needle had been to some extent utilized by Italian sailors in the twelfth century. But the early forms of the mariner's compass were too rough to be trusted on long voyages. Brunetto Latini (the tutor of Dante), who visited Roger Bacon at Oxford, probably in 1258, declared that its discovery "must remain concealed until other times, because no master-mariner dares to use it, lest he should fall under a supposition of his being a magician. Nor would even the sailors venture themselves out to sea under his command, if he took with him an instrument which carries so great an appearance of being constructed under the influence of some infernal spirit."

An advance was made during the following century, but the Portuguese historian Barros records with reference to one of Prince Henry's early expeditions, that the Portuguese mariners of that time were not accustomed thus to venture on the open sea, all their nautical knowledge being limited to coasting in sight of land." Prince Henry's instruments were a primitive astrolabe with a quadrant hung vertically from a ring held in the hand, and worked by the help of an alidade, "or ruled index having two holes pierced in its extremities through which the ray passed." Charts of any exact sort were almost confined to the Mediterranean: beyond Cape Non the conjectural outlines of the Christian mappe-monde failed to yield practical guidance.

If, in order to appreciate the position which India has held in the national life of Portugal, we must bear in mind the slow labour of the discovery, it is not less needful to understand the motives which sustained Prince Henry in his life's task. His chronicler, Azurara, explains that, apart from mere exploration, the prince greatly desired to abase the Moors, to establish trade with the west African coast, and to plant the Catholic faith among the heathen peoples there lying in a state of perdition. Grand Master of the Order of Christ, Prince Henry represented the Church Militant in Portugal as his order represented the crusading spirit of the Knights Templars to whose position and property in Portugal it had succeeded in the fourteenth century.

It was with his revenues as Grand Master that he defrayed the cost of his expeditions.

In 1454 King Affonso V of Portugal granted to the Order of Christ, in return for the discoveries thus made, the spiritual jurisdiction over Guinea, Nubia, and Ethiopia. A tribute of one-twentieth on all merchandise from Guinea, whether slaves or gold or whatever it might be, was secured to the Order of Christ by Prince Henry in 1458. The Portuguese nation was still deeply imbued with the crusading spirit. In 1458, two years before Prince Henry's death, when the Pope summoned the sovereigns of Europe against the Infidels, into whose hands Constantinople had fallen, Portugal made the most effective response. Prince Henry with twenty-five thousand men captured Alcaçar Seguer from the Moors, replying to their offer of surrender that "the king's object was the service of God, not to take their goods or force a ransom from them."

The three motives of Prince Henry – enmity to the Moslems, mercantile enterprise, and missionary zeal – profoundly influenced the whole history of the Portuguese in the East. As he aimed at outflanking the Moors in Africa by exploring down its western coast, so his greatest successors aimed at outflanking the Ottoman Empire by dominating the Red Sea. His commercial dealings on the African coast led to the slave-trade which poured an inexhaustible supply of cheap labour into Portugal, relieved the Portuguese from the tillage of the soil, and set free large numbers to carry Dut the royal policy of adventure beyond the sea. A heavy price of national exhaustion had to be afterwards paid for this spasm of external enterprise, but while it lasted the energy was intense. Prince Henry's third motive, proselytism, after a brilliant period of promise, crippled the Portuguese power in India and ended in the horrors of the Goa Inquisition.

Although the discoveries of Prince Henry were bounded by narrow limits, the impulse which he gave to discovery was decisive. He left behind him not only an astronomical observatory, a naval arsenal, and a great school of cartography and scientific navigation, but also a system of continuous exploration. His squadrons consisted of Portuguese ships sailed by Italian or Genoese pilots, and thus combined the nautical science of the Mediterranean with the hardy seamanship of the Atlantic. On his death his work was continued by three successive sovereigns of his house. They found that the Sea of Darkness was no black ocean after all. Prince Henry's improvements had freed long voyages from their worst dangers, and the Portuguese captains, having once rounded the exposed shoulder of north-western Africa, pushed south through less turbulent waters. In 1471 they passed the equator, and in 1484 they reached the Congo, erecting crosses wherever they landed down the African coast, and carving on trees Prince Henry's motto, Talent de bien faire, together with the name of the saint which they gave to the newly found land.

The great discoveries were taken possession of by an imposing ceremony. For example, having reached La Mina on January 19, 1482, "on the following morning they suspended the banner of Portugal from the bough of a lofty tree, at the foot of which they erected an altar, and the whole company assisted at the first mass that was celebrated in Guinea, and prayed for the conversion of the natives from idolatry, and the perpetual prosperity of the church which they intended to erect upon the spot." The baptism of a native prince, or of a few negroes seized or lured on board, seemed to the chroniclers of that age the crowning achievement of exploration.

At length in 1486 Bartholemeu Dias, of a family of daring navigators, rounded the southern point of Africa, but far out at sea in a tempest. He reached Algoa Bay on the eastern coast. There his crews lost heart and demanded an immediate return. After a few days' sail further north to the Great Fish River, Dias had to give up his chance of being the discoverer of India. Bidding a sad farewell to the cross which he had erected on the island of Santa Cruz, he turned back. On his way home he sighted the southern headland to which he gave the name of Cabo Tormentoso, the Cape of Storms, but which his master King John II rechristened the Cape of Good Hope, as a happy augury that the passage to India was now assured to his nation.

Meanwhile two episodes had occurred which determined the future course of maritime discovery. Columbus, during his stay in Portugal, 1470–1484, married the daughter of one of Prince Henry's commanders, and obtained access to his nautical journals, maps, and instruments. "It was in Portugal," writes Ferdinand Columbus of his illustrious father, "that the admiral began to surmise that if the Portuguese sailed so far south, one might also sail westwards and find land in that direction." This surmise was strengthened by the "Imago Mundi" of Cardinal Pierre d'Ailly, who had copied the passages which supplied the inspiration to Columbus almost word for word from Roger Bacon's "Opus Majus" written 143 years before. It received confirmation from the travels of Marco Polo, and from the chart and letter of Toscanelli which reached Columbus while at Lisbon.

Columbus had made up his mind, but the spirit of Prince Henry the Navigator no longer inspired the Portuguese counsels. The mathematical board, to whom the new king, John II, referred the project in 1482, discredited it on scientific grounds. The king himself had political reasons for doubting whether a western route to India, even if found, would be advantageous to Portugal. The map drawn (1457–1459), in the last years of Prince Henry's life, showed the way round the southern point of Africa up to Sofala and "Xengibar" on the east African coast. The subsequent discovery that the Gulf of Guinea trended almost due east seemed to disclose an even more direct course to India than was actually the case.

Not only did the southern route appear a certainty, but care had been taken to secure a monopoly of it for Portugal. The Bull of Pope Nicholas V in 1454 conferred on the Portuguese king all Guinea as far as a certain large river reputed to be the Nile, but which was really the Senegal. A western passage across the Atlantic to India might prove a dangerous rival to the almost discovered passage round the southern extremity of Africa. What between royal hesitations and scientific scepticism, Columbus found that little was to be hoped from Portugal (1481–1483). King John II listened to base counsels, and after trying to get a detailed plan from Columbus, sent out a secret expedition to secure the discovery on his own account. The surreptitious caravel was driven back by a storm, and in 1484 Columbus quitted Portugal in disgust, to hawk about a new world at incredulous courts during eight more weary years.

The other incident which affected the course of East Indian discovery is more honourable to Portugal. Azurara records that one of Prince Henry's main objects was to find out whether any Christian peoples dwelt in the unknown African world. The old confused tradition of a Christian potentate Prester John, and of a Christian nation in Ethiopia, had received confirmation from friars since Prince Henry's death. King John II of Portugal (1481–1495) resolved to seek out this lost Christian kingdom by sea and land. In August, 1486, he sent forth with that object the ships under Bartholemeu Dias, which, as we have seen, discovered the Cape of Good Hope, but which only proceeded up the east coast of Africa to a little beyond Algoa Bay. After an unsuccessful land mission by way of Jerusalem, John II despatched Pedro de Covilham and Alfonso de Paiva to gather information ,via Egypt about Prester John's country and the Indian Ocean. Covilham and Paiva started in May, 1487 (while Bartholemeu Dias was still absent on his sea expedition with the same purpose), and travelled by Naples, Rhodes, and Cairo to the Red Sea. At Aden they parted, Covilham sailing east in an Arab ship to the Indian coast and Paiva west to Abyssinia.

Covilham, the first Portuguese explorer in India, stayed some time on the Malabar coast and visited the very cities which were destined to become the centres of Portuguese activity. On his return voyage he touched at Sofala, the spot on the south-eastern coast of Africa marked on the Portuguese map of 1457–1459, and thus supplied the missing link between the sea discoveries round Africa and their ultimate goal in India. He also obtained some knowledge of the neighbouring island of Madagascar, known to the Moors as the Island of the Moon.

Charged with this all-important information Covilham hastened homewards, by way of the Red Sea. But at Cairo, on learning that his fellow traveller Paiva was dead, he himself proceeded to Ormuz and eventually to Abyssinia, the country of Prester John – where he married, rose to high office, and died after a residence of thirty-three years. Before leaving Cairo, however, in 1490, he sent home a report of his discoveries to the Portuguese king, with the pregnant message: "That the ships which sailed down the coast of Guinea might be sure of reaching the termination of the continent, by persisting in a course to the south; and that when they should arrive in the Eastern Ocean their best direction must be to inquire for Sofala and the Island of the Moon."

These striking words make Covilham the theoretical discoverer of the Cape route to India. They supplemented the news which Dias brought to Lisbon in December, 1487, of his having rounded the southern point of Africa. The pious zeal of the Portuguese sovereign in seeking for the unknown Christian country of Prester John was thus amply rewarded by land and by sea. Dias's discovery of the Cape passage toward India rendered John II uneasy lest Columbus's alternative route westward should be taken up by a rival power. On March 20, 1488, he accordingly wrote to Columbus at Seville, accepting the offer of the great navigator for the discovery of new continents. But Portugal had missed its chance. John IC, during the remaining seven years of his life, laboured amid sickness and domestic sorrow to strengthen his position on the African coast: Columbus in 1492 discovered for the Spanish crown the American islands which proved to be the outworks of a new world.

The discovery caused consternation at the Portuguese court. To the king it seemed that a short cut had been laid open to India: Columbus himself believed to his dying day that Cuba formed part of Asia. The Portuguese sovereign did not at first despair of snatching the fruits of the achievement. His treaty of Alcacora with Spain in 1479 had conceded to Portugal the exclusive right of navigation and discovery along the African coast, together with the possession of all known islands of the Atlantic save the Canaries. Columbus records that King John II affirmed in conversation with him the right of Portugal under this compact to the new Atlantic regions.

Meanwhile Columbus and his storm-tossed crew, having landed on their return voyage at St. Mary's Isle, February 18, 1493, were seized as prisoners by the Portuguese governor. Even after their release, and their reception in Portugal with outward marks of honour, it was proposed to make away with Columbus – another base counsel of courtiers which King John had this time the magnanimity to reject. Spain proved equally prompt. By the middle of April, 1493, Columbus was in the presence of Ferdinand and Isabella at Barcelona; and on May 3d, Pope Alexander VI, himself a Spaniard, granted three Privileges securing to their Catholic Majesties the exclusive right to the newly discovered lands.

This feat of diplomatic activity, hardly to be surpassed in our own time of telegraphs, was at once detected to have trenched on previous Papal grants to Portugal; and next day, May 4th, a Bull was issued to reconcile the conflicting titles. Spain was to have all lands discovered or to be discovered, and not occupied by any Christian prince at Christmas, 1492, to the west and south of an imaginary line one hundred leagues west and south of the Azores and the Cape Verde Islands, which the Bull vaguely takes as one group. No other nation was to sail thither for trade or any other purpose without permission of the Spanish crown.

Portugal objected to this line as too near to the African coast. After much negotiation, a dividing line between the two nations was fixed at 370 leagues west of the Cape Verde Islands by the Treaty of Tordesillas in 1494, and sanctioned by a Bull of Julius II in 1506. The final

Bull of Leo X in 1514, while confirming the previous one, gave to Portugal an exclusive right of discovery throughout the rest of the globe.

To Protestant writers these Papal proceedings have appeared in a somewhat distorted light – as the partition of an unknown world by a pontiff who had himself no title to it. In point of fact, they exhibit the normal action of international law and diplomacy as then established in Europe, and they formed the only course that could have been adopted, short of war. The Pope, if he no longer stood forth as the conscience of Christendom, represented after the fashion of that age what we now call the concert of Europe.

It is not needful to explore the pretensions of medieval Rome to the sovereignty of the world. By the time of Columbus such secular claims of Papal supremacy had narrowed themselves to two main functions: the settlement of disputes or the sanction of treaties between Christian princes, and the ratification of conquests or discoveries made in non-Christian lands. The annals of Spain and Portugal afford many examples of the exercise of this authority. Indeed, the recognition of the Portuguese as a political entity dates from the Bull of Alexander III in 1179 affirming their independence. Their exclusive right to the discoveries made by Prince Henry the Navigator and his successors in the fifteenth century rested on a similar international basis. In 1454 Pope Nicholas V authorized Portugal to invade and conquer all infidel or pagan countries, and to enslave their inhabitants. Any one infringing on this grant was to fall under the wrath of God and of the Blessed Apostles Peter and Paul. After reciting the zeal and labours of Prince Henry, his Holiness granted as a perpetual possession to Portugal all lands discovered or to be discovered south of Capes Non and Bojador. The Bull of Sixtus IV in 1481 assigned the spiritual jurisdiction of these countries from Cape Bojador usque ad Indos to the Portuguese Order of Christ. Such instruments were then the title-deeds of nations.

In these grants the Popes merely exercised an authority regarded in that age as essential to the peace of Christendom. When therefore the discoveries of Columbus raised rival claims between Spain and Portugal, both parties sought the decision of Rome as to how much of the unknown world had already been assigned to Portugal, and as to what remained available to Spain. Pope Alexander VI, the whole Sacred College consenting, at first acted hastily on the representations of Spain; he amended his decision the next day, perhaps on the representation of Portugal; and the theoretical line of demarcation could be shown authoritatively on the chart only after years of nautical research and diplomatic wrangling.

By the Treaty of Tordesillas, between Spain and Portugal, June 7, 1494, each nation was to despatch one or two caravels to the Canaries with pilots and "astrologers" to mark off 370 leagues west of the Cape Verde Islands. Apart from international intrigues, the first essential toward the ascertainment of the line, namely the verified measurement of a degree on a great circle, was not arrived at till a century and a half later, in 1669. The line appears on the Cantino map of 1502, but a precise determination of longitude, on which the demarcation depended, was beyond the resources of that age.

Such questions of detail did not materially affect the authority of the Papal award; all the sovereigns at that time within the concert of Christendom accepted the Pope's partition of the unknown world between Portugal and Spain. Even princes, like our later Tudors, who renounced their spiritual allegiance to Rome, shrank for a time from openly assailing a political settlement which had become part of the public law of Europe.

I have dwelt on that settlement, because it explains much that has hitherto been obscure, and not a little that has hitherto seemed unreasonable, in the action of European nations in Asia. It enables us to understand how the Portuguese came habitually to speak of all India as their own, although they never possessed more than a few petty settlements on its coast. It throws light on the long hesitation of Protestant England before she struck boldly into the Indian seas on her own account. It legally justified the stigma of piracy affixed by Spain and Portugal to our intrusion within their demarcated line. While the Dutch East India Company were "rebeldes," as representing the Protestant revolt against Spain, the English East India Company were "piratas," as representing the Protestant intrusion on the Papal settlement of the unknown world. This term still clings to the English in the Portuguese memory, and was revived against us during the strained relations of 1891. Even the British sovereigns, which long formed the chief gold currency of Portugal, were popularly known as "piratas."

It may seem as if the rounding of the Cape by Dias in 1487, and Covilham's instructions in 1490 for completing the route to India, should at once have opened up Asia to Portugal. But in 1490 King John II was seized by the lingering malady, supposed to have been caused by drinking poisoned water, which overshadowed the rest of his life. On his partial recovery in 1491 he had to lament the death of his only son; his queen was attacked by a sickness, almost mortal, in 1493; and the afflicted monarch struggled through a renewal of his illness only to find his kingdom devastated by famine in 1494, and to die in October, 1495. His successor, Emmanuel the Fortunate, at once revived the long-suspended plan of Indian discovery. In 1496 preparations were made on a scale never before attempted, and in July, 1497, Vasco da Gama sailed from the little chapel on the Tagus, which Prince Henry had built for administering the sacrament to outward-bound and home-returning mariners.

In the preceding month of May, 1497, John Cabot embarked from the Severn with a crew of eighteen men to seek for India westwards across the Atlantic. On June 24th, or exactly a fortnight before Da Gama left Lisbon, Cabot discovered North America for England instead.

Da Gama's squadron, insignificant as it may appear to modern seamen, marked a century of progress since Prince Henry's day of small things. Even as late as 1486 Bartholemeu Dias went forth to round the Cape of Good Hope with only two ships of fifty tons each and a provision tender. Da Gama's fleet in 1497 consisted of the San Gabriel of 120 tons carrying his own flag, the San Raphael of one hundred tons commanded by his brother, a caravel of fifty tons, and a smaller craft laden with munitions. Nor was the improvement in their equipment less striking. Considerable difficulties exist in tracing the early development of the rig of ships. But Columbus enumerates all his sails on October 24, 1492 – a fair supply; and drawings exist, if we could but be sure they were authentic, of Da Lama's two ships and caravel. They were built of carefully chosen wood, strongly fastened with iron, carried 160 men, and each had a triple store of sails, spars, and rope. The improvement of the astrolabe by Martin Behaim in 1480 gave Da Gama facilities for navigation unknown to Prince Henry, nor were his nautical instruments as a whole inadequate.

Vasco da Gama finally sailed from the Tagus on Saturday, July 8, 1497, reached Calicut on the Indian coast on May 20, 1498, and returned to Lisbon in August or September, 1499: successful indeed, but having lost his brother, half his ships, and more than half his crew. That memorable voyage has a whole literature of its own. It supplied the national epic of Portugal and many a glowing page to the Portuguese historians. It has been examined and re-examined by modern nautical critics. It is made to move afresh before our eyes by one of the most picturesque, yet most practical, travellers of our time – Sir Richard Francis Burton, in his work on Camoens and the Lusiad. Da Gama not only found the way from the Cape of Good Hope over the Indian Sea, but he shaped his course direct through mid-ocean from the Cape Verde Islands to the Cape of Good Hope, and thus made the first passage across the South Atlantic.

The expedition, like those of Prince Henry and his royal successors in exploration, was the work of the Portuguese dynasty rather than of the Portuguese people. King Emmanuel gave from his own hand to Vasco da Gama the banner of the squadron, embroidered with the cross of the military Order of Christ. The Council of State was almost unanimous against the enterprise, and the popular clamour burst forth as the ships sailed from the shore. This clamour, which had from time to time been raised against the royal policy of Indian exploration during the previous eighty years, finds a mouthpiece in the imprecations which close the fourth book of the Lusiad.

Camoens vrrote in the generation immediately succeeding the events which he described, and was intimately acquainted with the contemporary feeling in regard to them. He makes a venerable figure arise, with arm. waved to heaven as the ships set sail, and denounce the madness of a monarch who, with an enemy at his gates, seeks the meteor fame of conquest in an unknown world. This dynastic as opposed to a popular impulse forms the key to the Portuguese history in India. One attempt after another by the crown to hand over the Indian trade to public enterprise failed. It may be doubted, indeed, whether any European people in the fifteenth century had the cohesion or steadfast-ness necessary to carry out the explorations which ended in the discovery of the Cape route to India, except under pressure from a line of resolute kings. It is certain that the Italian republics had not. But it is equally certain that, in spite of the devotion of Portuguese sovereigns and the heroism of the Portuguese chivalry, the curse of the weird prophet of the Lusiad, amid whose maledictions Da Gama departed, in the end came true – the prize a shadow or a rainbow blaze.

The expedition struck, however, a chord of Portuguese national feeling. Both king and people regarded it as a continuation of the Crusades: a crusade on a larger scale and with better prospects of plunder. Camoens opens the seventh book of his Lusiad by reproaching Germany, England, France, and Italy for their coldness to the sacred cause, calls them once more to Holy War, and shames their silence by declaring that Portugal will single-handed fight the battle of God. His contempt for these Gallios of Christendom is only equalled by his hatred of the Moslems and his travesty of their faith. In the mythological machinery of the Lusiad, Bacchus stands forth as the genius of Islam while Venus pleads the cause of the Christians. Bacchus appears to a priest of the Koran in the form of Mohammed – the founder of a religion of abstinence from wine! No doubt Camoens had in his mind the celestial Venus and the Indian Bacchus. His ignorance of the Moslem creed is as complete as his confidence in his own. The noble Portuguese cavalier would no more inquire into the truth of his religion than into the honour of his mistress. He might know nothing about either, but he was equally convinced of both. This confidence, light-hearted yet profound, led alike to the success and to the failure of the Portuguese in India. It plunged them into military enterprises, rendered glorious by acts of individual valour, but far beyond their collective strength. It impelled them on a career of religious proselytism, illustrated by beautiful examples of personal piety, yet ending in political atrocities which left an indelible stain on the Christian cause.

The missionary spirit of the military Order of Christ, with the sword in its hand and the Cross on its banner, had animated its Grand Master Prince Henry and the sovereigns of his house who, during eighty years (1418–1498), carried out the work of continuous discovery. It burned in Da Gama's breast as he fell on his knees in sight of the Indian shore. It breathes in the prophetic strains of the tenth book of the Lusiad, and in that magnificent vision of a Christian Indian empire which the Portuguese, as the heaven-sent successors of St. Thomas, were to build up. It excuses the exaggerated view of Portuguese historians in regard to their real position in India, and their perpetual confusion of personal heroism with political achievement.

The epic of Vasco da Gama is an allegory of his nation's story in the East. His last night on shore he watched in prayer at the chapel of Belem like a true Crusader, commending himself and his cause to God. He commenced his voyage amid royal honours and popular misgivings; he conducted it with undaunted courage to success; he returned in a blaze of triumph – amid which he himself crept away to a lonely retreat on the beach, to mourn for the brother and brave comrades buried on far-off shores or gone down in the mighty waters.

Chapter 3 – The Struggle Between Christendom and Islam for the Indian Seas

1509–1600

The Portuguese landing was fortunate both as to place and time. The India which Da Gama reached in 1498 was not the great empire of the Moghuls, but a narrow shore-strip shut out from the rest of the continent by a mountain wall, and itself partitioned among petty rajas. The two ranges of the eastern and the western Ghats which run down the opposite coasts of the peninsula, have from time immemorial determined its political geography. The eastern Ghats stretch fragmentary spurs and ridges along the Madras side, receding far inland and leaving broad tracts between their base and the sea. This open region, everywhere available for civilized settlement, became the seat of the ancient kingdoms of southern India. The western Ghats, on the other hand, form the sea-buttresses of the Bombay presidency, with a contracted space, sometimes a mere palm-tree fringe, between them and the shore. At places they rise in magnificent cliffs and headlands out of the ocean, and justify their name as the colossal "landing-stairs" from the deep.

It was on this shut-off western coast that the Portuguese alighted, and it was destined to remain the sole theatre of their conquests within India. Its chief port, Calicut, off which Da Gama anchored in May, 1498, was the capital of one of many rajas who had seized the fragments of the prehistoric kingdom of Chera. According to native tradition the last Hindu sovereign of Chera, on his conversion to Islam in the ninth century A.D., had divided out his dominions and piously sailed for Medina.

The main part of his territories went to form the Hindu kingdom of Vijayanagar in the interior of the peninsula. Out of the residue, Mussulman adventurers from the north carved for themselves inland states, which had coalesced under the Bahmanid dynasty in the fourteenth and fifteenth centuries A.D. The coast-strip of Malabar, excluded from these larger kingdoms by the mountain wall of the Ghats, was left to be scuffled for by seaport rajas, of whom the Zamorin of Calicut became the chief. The size of Calicut may be inferred from the legend that it took its name, Koli-Kukkuga, "Cock-crowing," or Koli-kotta, "Cock-Fort," because its limits had been fixed at the distance at which the crowing of a cock in the chief temple could be heard. Its ruler, although supported by allies or mercenaries dwelling among the hills, derived his importance from ocean commerce, and bore the title of Zamorin, literally the Sea-Raja, Zamorin being a European form of the Tamil Scimari, which is still used in official addresses to the Calicut chief, and is traceable to a Sanskrit patronymic Samudri, meaning "Son of the Sea."

The Portuguese might have searched India in vain for a spot better suited to their purpose. Their three objects were conquest, commerce, and conversion. For each of these three objects, the Malabar coast-strip afforded free scope. Its chiefs were too petty to resist even a small European Power. They welcomed foreign merchants, as the greater part of their revenues consisted of dues on sea-trade. They allowed liberty of religion in their little shore domains, and they were accustomed to a local population of Jews and Christians whose political existence in India dated from a period more ancient than their own.

As regards the power of the coast-rajas, even the most important of them, Calicut and Cochin, were merely two among half a dozen patches of the Malabar strip; all Malabar had formed but one-eighth of the single kingdom of Kerala; and the entire kingdom of Kerala was only one of the fifty-six countries of India recognized by Hindu geography. After Kerala broke up, its largest fragment, Vijayanagar, was reported with Eastern exaggeration to have "three hundred ports, each one of which is equal to Calicut." The Portuguese were themselves on so small a scale that they may well be excused if they overestimated the importance of the princelets with whom they came in contact. Their whole view of their territorial conquests within India was, in truth, out of perspective.

Affonso de Albuquerque in 1507, when the Portuguese had but two or three little forts on the Indian coast, spoke of his master in diplomatic correspondence as "King of Portugal and Lord of the Indies." The Indian titles assumed by the Portuguese sovereigns, and further exaggerated by their courtiers, were yet more absurdly grandiose. The overestimates of the Lusiad may plead the license of poetry, but even the Lisbon dictionary-maker rises in flights of fancy when he touches an Indian word. The name of that respectable coast-chief, the Zamorin, is explained by Bluteau to mean "Supreme emperor and God upon earth." The Portuguese conquests on the Indian continent were never equal in extent to one of the hundred divisions of the Moghul empire, nor ever contained the average population of a single one of the 250 British Indian districts of our day. The real "India Portugueza" was the dominion of the Eastern seas, a mighty achievement for so small a nation.

The isolated coast-rajas of Malabar were not only on a scale with which Portugal could fairly cope, but they gladly opened their harbours to strangers. Those harbours, sometimes mere roadsteads, had formed the regular meeting marts of Indo-European commerce from prehistoric times. After touching at Ceylon the junks from farther Asia met the Arab ships at Quilon, Cochin, Calicut, and Cannanore, all on the Malabar strip. Even the merchantmen from Egypt, who traded direct with Ceylon and Malacca, usually crept up the Malabar shore before striking across the Indian Ocean to the Persian Gulf and the Red Sea. Malabar had thus an unbroken policy of commerce with the West, more ancient even than its appearance in Indicopleustes as "Male, where the pepper grows." If the Peutingerian Tables represent the facts about 226 A.D., Rome had two cohorts stationed at Cranganore (now called Kodungalur) on the Malabar coast to protect her trade at that early date, and had already erected a local temple to Augustus. In the heroics of the seventh canto of the Lusiad as rendered by Sir Richard Burton:

"Great is the country, rich in every style

Of goods from China sent by sea to Nyle."

The Malabar chiefs were tolerant of the religions of the many nations who traded at their ports. Indeed, the native population itself professed widely diverse forms of faith. Hinduism, which made northern India its own, had more slightly impressed itself on that secluded southern coast. The lower classes and hill-tribes still clung to their primitive pre-Hindu rites; the military race of Nairs proudly asserted, as they still assert, their non-Hindu system of family life and inheritance. The chiefs were either semi-Hindus or manufactured into high-caste Hindus on their accession to the throne – as at least one of them is to this day. The strictly Hindu element was a small one, made up of Brahmans whose ancestors had brought their faith from the north, or of subsequent converts. But although few in numbers the Brahmans held a conspicuous place as holy men and as councillors of the rajas.

This religious freedom was characteristic from early times of the emporiums along the Asiatic sea-route. Abu Zaid of Siraf, when mentioning the foreign colonies in Ceylon (circ. 916 A.D.), records that "the king allows each sect to follow its own religion." Manichmans, Mussulmans, Jews, and Christians were alike welcome at the Malabar ports. The coast-rajas had specially favoured religions of the Messianic type. If the connection of the Malabar Jews with Solomon's fleets must be relegated to legend, traditions carry back their arrival to their escape from servitude under Cyrus in the sixth century B.C. They tell how later colonies came after the final destruction of the Temple, bringing with them the silver jubilee trumpets. A copper grant proves that they were recognized by the Chera sovereign as self-governing communities at the beginning of the eighth century A.D. These prehistoric Jewish settlements formed in the time of Da Gama, and continue to form at this day, a distinctive feature of the southwest Indian seaboard.

Even more important were the Nestorian communities of St. Thomas Christians, whom the Portuguese found both numerous and powerful on the coast of Malabar. They took their name of "St. Thomas Christians" from the tradition that the Doubting Apostle had preached throughout India and obtained the seal of martyrdom near Madras in 68 A.D. (although the accuracy of the tradition is doubted by some)1, and they preserved under a broken succession of bishops an early Asiatic form of the faith. Metal plates attest their existence as organized communities in the eighth and ninth centuries A.D. These Malabar Christian and Jewish grants, flotsam of the wreckage of perhaps a thousand years, are written in a long disused primitive alphabet known as Vatteluttu of the Malayalam language. The St. Thomas Christians enjoyed a rank equal in name at any rate to the Nairs, and are said, like them, to have supplied soldiers to the coast-rajas. They also held office in the great Hindu court of the interior. In 1442 an Indian Christian acted as prime minister to the King of Vijayanagar – the suzerain Hindu State of southern India.

The Arab traders found the same friendly reception at the Malabar ports after their conversion to Islam as in their old Saban days. Their name of Mappillas, or Moplahs, was an honourable one, apparently in ancient times shared with the Christians. Those now fiercely bigoted Mussulmans were in the time of Da Gama composed of two classes: descendants of early Arabian settlers who took the mild Indian view of other faiths; and recent arrivals from Egypt or the Persian Gulf, inflamed with religious hatred which the Crusades had fanned, and to which the fall of. the Grenada Saracens added fresh fury. This distinction between the old Arab settlers in Malabar and the foreign population of traders from Arabia must be borne in mind. The coast-rajas and their native subjects were pleased to do business with newcomers, whatever their creed. But the Arab and Portuguese strangers brought with them an explosive fanaticism always ready to blow religious toleration into the air. An avowed object of the greatest of the Indo-Portuguese governors, Albuquerque, 1509–1515, was to strip the shrine of Mecca and carry off the body of the False Prophet, with a view to ransoming the Holy Temple of Jerusalem in exchange. In his Letters and Commentaries, as in the Papal Bulls, the struggle between Christendom and Islam, and the crusading spirit of the Portuguese, stand revealed.

If the Portuguese were fortunate as to their place of landing in India, they were even more so in the time of their arrival. The great Hindu overlordship of Seringapatam is a town of some ten thousand inhabitants and is situated in the Mysore District of Southern India. It was once the capital of the rajas of Mysore, but it fell before the English at the end of the eighteenth century and yielded its prestige as capital to the city of Mysore itself. The great temple of Vishnu Sri Ranga, with its towering front rising tier after tier, is one of the noteworthy sites of Seringapatam.

Vijayanagar in the interior was beset by the newer Mussulman kingdoms, and had no leisure for the petty politics of the coast-strip. In 1564 Vijayanagar finally went down before the Moslems on the field of Talikot after an existence of four and a half centuries. Its capital can still be traced far inland in the Madras District of Bellary – vast ruins of temples, fortifications, reservoirs and bridges, with a remnant of 693 human beings amid a population composed of hyenas, jackals, and snakes.

At the coming of Vasco da Gama the Mussulman kingdoms of the south were also in the throes of dissolution and new birth. The Balunanid dynasty, formed from the coalition of the Mussulman adventurers in the fourteenth century, began to break up in 1489, and by 1525 its disintegration was complete. The Portuguese arrived just as this once powerful kingdom was evolving itself through internecine wars into the Five Mussulman States of southern India. Four of the five cared nothing for the isolated coast-strip outside their mountain wall. . The fifth intervened only when stung by insult; and its intervention was cut short by the distractions incident to the succession of a boy-prince.

The inland Hindu kingdom and the five inland Mussulman states of southern India, although more powerful than any of the coast chiefs such as the Zamorin of Calicut, were themselves insignificant compared with the great powers of the north. But at that time the Afghan sovereignty in northern India was dwindling to the vanishing point. The invasion of Tamerlane in 1398–1399 had left the Delhi monarchy in ruins, and the next century passed in flickering attempts to revive it. Some of the Delhi Sultans ruled only a few miles around their capital. Hindu princes and Mussulman soldiers of fortune set up for themselves, till at length in 1526 the Moghul invasion from Central Asia swept away the wreck of the old Indo-Moslem dynasties. Yet another thirty years of feebleness elapsed before the accession of Akbar, the real founder of the Moghul empire. When Vasco da Gama landed in 1498 the old order of things alike in northern and in southern India was passing away, the new order had not yet emerged.

The Portuguese, therefore, found a free hand in dealing with the petty coast chiefs. The Zamorin of Calicut received them graciously and looked forward to an increased customs-revenue from their trade. But the foreign Arab merchants, then the most powerful community at his port, perceived that the new ocean-route must imperil their ancient monopoly by way of the Red Sea. They accordingly incited the court officials to intrigues which nearly ended in a treacherous massacre. At length Da Gama departed with rich cargoes, presents, and a letter from the Zamorin to the Portuguese king proposing an interchange of commerce. On the passage up the coast, before striking west for Africa, Da Gama lay in at Cannanore. Here the raja, being on a still smaller scale than the Zamorin, is said to have loaded the Portuguese with gifts – "more spices and merchandise than the vessels could hold" – and signed with his own hand a treaty of friendship written on gold leaf.

The return of Da Gallia to Lisbon in 1499 with a freight which repaid sixty times the cost of the expedition, called forth an outburst of mercantile enthusiasm such as had never thrilled a European nation.

It seemed as if the Portuguese king and people were come into a sudden fortune beyond the seas. King Emmanuel, after loading Da Gama with wealth and honours, assumed the dignity of "Lord of the Conquest, Navigation, and Commerce of Ethiopia, Arabia, Persia, and India." His claim to possess the non-Christian world to the east of the Atlantic dividing line was perfectly clear from the point of view of European public law. It had been solemnly granted by Papal Bulls and ratified by Spanish treaties. Pope Alexander VI by a further Bull in 1502 confirmed the new style of Lord of the Conquest of India, etc., which the Portuguese king added to his titles.

The monopoly of Indian dominion and trade, thus legally secured to Portugal, was interpreted by her in no illiberal spirit. It appeared in some sense as a trust which she held for Christendom. In 1500 the king declared the commerce with India "which by the grace of God our Lord we discovered and hold in our power" to be open on equal terms "to all our natives and likewise to the foreigners who are in our kingdoms and who hold our letters-of naturalization." The terms were that the ships employed should be of at least two hundred tons burden, and should pay to the royal treasury one-fourth of what "in good time they should bring in return." This charter was to hold for two years, and although many changes, not for the better, afterward took place, the Portuguese system during the next half-century allowed other Christian nations to profit at Lisbon by the Indian trade – an opportunity of which English merchants largely availed themselves.

King Emmanuel lost no time in trying to convert his claims to the "Conquest of India" into a reality. In 1500 he despatched a fleet of thirteen ships strongly armed with artillery, manned by the boldest sailors, and steered by the most skilful pilots of the time. It also carried an abundant provision for proselytism in eight Franciscan friars, eight chaplains, and a chaplain-major. Its commander, Pedro Alvarez Cabral, after discovering Brazil on the way out, was well received by the Zamorin at Calicut. With his sanction the Portuguese established a factory, or agency-house, on shore for the purchase of spices. After capturing an Arab ship off the roadstead as a present to the prince, Cabral hastened the somewhat tardy collection of cargo by seizing a Moslem vessel in the harbour. These lessons in the Christian methods of armed trade made the foreign Arab merchants realize that the struggle between them and the Portuguese was for life or death. They sacked the Portuguese factory, or trading post, at Calicut, slaying the chief agent and fifty-three of his men. Cabral retorted by destroying ten Arab ships, and sailed down the coast to Cochin, burning two more Calicut vessels on his way.

Cochin, a rival port to Calicut, loaded his fleet with spices on fair terms. Cabral signed a treaty with the local raja, promised to make him some day Zamorin of Calicut, and established a house of agency on shore with a factor and six assistants to provide cargo for the next ships from Portugal. Friendly overtures from the neighbouring coast-rajas of Quilon and Cannanore, with a visit to the latter roadstead, proved that there were plenty of trading-places besides Calicut on the Malabar seaboard. Unfortunately Cabral carried off, he says by accident, a hostage who had come temporarily on board at Cochin. To the honour of Indian clemency be it recorded that the raja took no reprisals against the defenceless Portuguese factors left in his power. Cabral returned to Lisbon in July, 1501, with a rich freight, but having lost seven of his thirteen ships in distant and tempestuous seas.

Before his arrival the king had sent forth, in April, 1501, another squadron of four vessels under João da Nova, who pursued the same system of plundering and burning the Calicut ships and laying in freight at the rival Malabar ports where the foreign Arabs were either not so numerous or more under control.

The experience gained by Cabral formed the starting-point of the Portuguese policy in the East. King Emmanuel had the choice between peaceful trade at half a dozen Malabar roadsteads or an armed monopoly founded on the coercion of the chief port, Calicut, and the destruction of the Arab commerce. He chose the armed monopoly. Cabral took the first step by leaving behind a factory at Cochin – a measure on which Da Gama had not ventured at any Indian port, and which involved a protective system of some kind. At first it seemed as if the protection could be secured by a Portuguese squadron in Indian waters and by severe reprisals for injuries done to factories on shore. Accordingly in the spring of 1502 the king sent forth a great fleet of twenty ships under Vasco da Gama as Admiral of the Indian Seas, with instructions to leave five caravels to guard the Malabar coast.

Da Gama's first voyage in 1497–1499 had been one of discovery: the object of his second was to secure a permanent foothold on the Indian coast for armed commerce. In both cases he thoroughly accomplished his task. On his second expedition in 1502, he bombarded Calicut and destroyed its Arab merchant-fleet. At four other of the Malabar ports (Cochin, Cannanore,

Quilon, and Baticala – the latter lying north of Cannanore) he established close commercial relations and left behind factories at two of them, together with a squadron under his flag-captain as Captain-Major of the Indian Sea. At one factory, Cannanore, he landed garrison-guns, balls, and gunpowder by permission of the raja, but buried them out of sight to avoid offence to the natives.

Da Gama's successes were, however, stained by cruelties never to be forgotten. On capturing the Calicut fleet he cut off the hands, ears, and noses of the crews, eight hundred men, and sent them, heaped up with dry leaves, to the raja to make a curry of. The teeth of the prisoners were beaten down their throats with staves. A Brahman messenger was compelled to confess himself a spy under the torture of live coals. His lips and ears were cut off, the ears of a dog – an unclean animal – were sewn to his head, and the mutilated wretch was returned to the Zamorin. Da Gama's flag-captain, Vincente Sodre, revenged some insulting words, real or imaginary, of which the Cannanore raja complained, by flogging the chief Arab merchant of the place till he fainted, filling his mouth with dirt, and tying over it a piece of bacon.

Da Gama returned a second time triumphant to Lisbon in 1503. But he left the Zamorin and the Arab mer-chants burning to avenge the tortures and outrages he had inflicted. They attacked the Cochin raja, seized his capital, and demanded the surrender of the Portuguese factors left under his protection. The Cochin chief bravely held out in spite of defeats and distresses until relieved by the arrival of the next fleet from Portugal in September, 1503.

Two divisions of that fleet under Affonso de Albuquerque and his cousin Francisco de Albuquerque laid the foundation of the shore defences of the Portuguese in India. The third division under Antonio Saldanha explored the east African coast, plundering and burning such Moorish craft as it met right up to the Red Sea, and thus initiated the policy of cutting off the Indian Mussulman trade from its Egyptian base. The squadron left behind under Da Gama's flag-captain Sodre had in the same year, 1503, carried the war into the enemy's waters. After cruising for a time along the Malabar coast, to protect the Portuguese factories, Sodre struck across the Indian Ocean to intercept the Egyptian traders as they passed out of the Red Sea, but he was wrecked off Socotra and perished together with three ships. In India the two Albuquerques built a fort at Cochin by consent of the raja whom they had rescued from the clutch of Calicut, established a new factory at Quilon, and severely punished the Zamorin. In his agreements with the coast chiefs, Affonso was careful to secure the ancient rights of the St. Thomas Christians, and a chapter of his Commentaries is devoted to the subject. At Quilon he insisted "that the civil and criminal jurisdiction should be under the control of the native Christians as it had always been hitherto," and commanded the Portuguese factor, or agent, whom he left behind "to act in all things conformably to their counsel." Affonso de Albuquerque, after quarrelling with his cousin Francisco, returned to Lisbon with a rich cargo in July, 1504: Francisco was lost on his way home, together with the squadron under his command.

Their departure gave the signal for renewed hostilities by the Zamorin against Cochin. But Duarte Pacheco, the captain of Albuquerque's lately erected fort, with its garrison of one hundred to 150 Portuguese and three hundred native soldiers, feebly aided by the Cochin levies, beat back all attacks, and finally routed the Zamorin's huge forces by land and sea. Pacheco thus showed in 1503–1504 that the Portuguese position could best be secured by supporting one rival raja. against another and by strengthening a small body of Europeans with disciplined native troops under European command. For the recruitment of such troops good materials existed among the brave military caste of Nairs, the Malabar Christians, and the old Mussulman settlers, who had little sympathy with the bigoted newcomers from Arabia and Egypt.

The Hindu Zamorin began to realize his mistake in allowing himself to be dragged into opposition to the Portuguese by the fanatical Arab traders at his harbour. Pacheco gave an equally useful lesson at Quilon, where the Arabs tried to force the Hindu queen into a similar antagonism. The gallant Pacheco, who had so splendidly maintained the cause of his country against overwhelming odds, was on his return to Lisbon received with royal smiles, and his achievements were preached in every church throughout Portugal. He was then imprisoned on false charges and was released only to live in distress and to die in penury.

The next expedition under Lopo Soarez de Albergaria, in 1504, consisted of thirteen of the largest ships ever built in Portugal. It continued the policy of unsparing destruction against the ports in which the Arab influence prevailed; laid part of Calicut in ruins; burned Cranganore and all the vessels in its harbour, sparing only the houses and churches of the St. Thomas Christians. The richer and more prudent among the Arab traders, hopeless of protection by the coast-rajas against the yearly squadrons from Portugal, put their remaining wealth on board a great flotilla to carry them back to the Persian Gulf and Egypt. But Soarez caught the rich fleet before it could escape, captured seventeen of its ships, slew two thousand men, and broke the Arab supremacy on the Malabar coast.

During the six years since Da Gama had returned to Lisbon in 1499, Portuguese commerce had passed through four stages. First: the original plan was to regard the ships as floating factories which should buy up spices at the Indian ports and convey them to Lisbon. Second: in 1500–1501 Cabral established a permanent agency on shore; in 1502 Da Gama's second expedition increased the shore agencies, and made secret provision for their defence. Third: in 1503 Albuquerque no longer thought it needful to bury the Portuguese cannon underground, and turned the Cochin agency into a fortified factory with a garrison of European and native soldiers under Portuguese officers, while his colleague Saldanha struck at the base of the Arab trade at the mouth of the Red Sea. Fourth: in 1504–1505, Pacheco and Soarez dealt a decisive blow to the Arab interest at the South Indian ports, cut off the retreat of the Arab traders to the Persian Gulf, and secured to Portugal the command of the Malabar waters.

History, ancient or modern, records no achievement of armed commerce so rapid, so brilliant, and so fraught with lasting results. Portugal in the first enthusiasm of her great discovery had, under a resolute monarch, put forth all her strength. Not only the Moslem world, but also the Mediterranean republics, woke up to find a new power established in India which was destroying their Eastern trade by way of the Red Sea. The results of that awakening, and the unholy coalitions between Venetian and Turk which it brought about, will presently appear. King Emmanuel perceived that he had a task on his hands, and perils impending, with which his yearly system of armed merchant fleets was unable to cope.

The absence of a permanent Portuguese head in India had led to abuses and gave a temporary character to the most brilliant victories. "If your Highness does not send us aid all will be lost," the agent at Cochin wrote on the rumoured coming of a Turkish fleet in 1504. "I further certify to your Highness that if we had in this land one who should govern us as is due we should have for your service, your Highness might well sleep soundly, and so long as this be not so, believe me, the very governors themselves are the very Rumes (Turks), both for the land and for the Fidalgos who serve in her." King Emmanuel resolved on a change of policy which would remove all doubts as to the permanence of the Portuguese stay on the Malabar coast and as to his determination to hold what his fleets and soldiers won. In March, 1505, he sent forth Dom Francisco da Almeida, a nobleman of illustrious rank, with a force such as had never sailed to India, and with instructions to assume the title of Viceroy on his arrival.

The task assigned to the first Christian Viceroy of India was threefold. As the Portuguese occupation was to be permanent, Almeida was firmly to secure the base on the east African coast, whence the fleets started across the Indian Ocean to Malabar. This he did by erecting a strong fort at Quiloa, or Kilwa, in Africa, by reducing Mombassa, on the north of Zanzibar, to dependence, by drawing tighter the Portuguese hold on Melinde, still further north, near the Bay of Formosa, and by establishing a Portuguese pilot service for the Indian seas. Having thus secured the strategic command of the Zanzibar coast from Mozambique up to the equator, Almeida proceeded to the second part of his task – the coercion of the Malabar ports at which the foreign Arabs still struggled for the upper hand, and the strengthening of the Portuguese factories on shore. His third duty was to break the Moslem power at sea, not alone the armed merchantmen of Calicut, but the regular navy with which the Mamluk Sultan of Egypt now menaced the existence of Portugal in the East.

If the Portuguese feats of arms in India had been brilliant, the policy which directed and supported them at Lisbon was far-reaching and profound. King Emmanuel discerned that it was no longer a question of destroying the Arab commerce on the Malabar coast or of intercepting it at the mouth of the Red Sea. It had become a struggle for the command of the whole Indian Ocean – the third and last act in the long conflict between medieval Christendom and Islam. In the central arena of that conflict, Palestine and the Byzantine Empire, the Moslems remained the victors after centuries of fighting. In its western arena, Spain and Portugal, Christendom had tardily triumphed. The battle-ground was now to be shifted to the Far East. The great Moslem powers realized this fact as clearly as King Emmanuel himself.

It was in vain, however, that the Mamluk Sultan of Egypt threatened to slay all Christians and demolish the Holy Sepulchre, if the Pope did not stop Portuguese aggression in the East. In vain, too, the Venetians, who found their trade by way of Egypt imperilled, joined the Sultan in trying to frighten his Holiness into putting pressure on the Court of Lisbon. The Pope was somewhat frightened; King Emmanuel not at all. To the Papal representations his Majesty piously replied that his Indian policy tended to the propagation of the Faith and to the extension of the Holy See. He knew that he had turned the flank of Islam, and that he had the sympathy of Catholic Europe in this final and greatest of the Crusades.

The force entrusted to Almeida was on a scale adequate to the work to be done. Twenty-two ships, of which thirteen were to remain on guard in India, carried with them a huge store of munitions of war and 1500 soldiers besides their crews. In four years (1505–1509) Almeida and his gallant son Lourenço overthrew the remaining power of the Arabs at the Malabar ports and defeated another great effort of the Zamorin at sea, destroying his fleet of eighty-four ships and 120 galleys and slaying three thousand Mussulmans. In 1506 Lourenço carried the Portuguese influence southward to Ceylon and received the homage of the native prince to the King of Portugal. The Ceylonese ruler agreed to pay a tribute of cinnamon and elephants, in return for which the Portuguese were to defend him against all enemies.

Meanwhile Egypt was arming. The. Mamluk Sultan, finding Venetian intrigues and papal remonstrances alike powerless to stay the Portuguese progress, sent forth in 1508 a great expedition under Admiral Amir Husain (the Mir Hogem or Mir Hozem of the Portuguese records), with instructions to effect a coalition with the Indian Mussulman sea powers. The junction with the Moslem fleet of the northern Bombay coast had already been made, when Lourenço Almeida was ordered with a few ships to prevent their further union with the remnant of the Calicut, or southern, squadron.

All he could do was to throw himself across their path, and at the price of his own life to give his father time to gather the Portuguese forces. A cannon-shot broke the young hero's leg at the first onset, but he had himself placed on a chair at the foot of the mainmast, and continued quietly to issue his orders till a second ball shattered his breast. The Moslem victors gave him honourable burial and respectfully congratulated Almeida on a son who, at the age of twenty-two, had covered himself with imperishable glory.

In the following spring, 1509, Almeida in person defeated the combined Moslem fleets off Diu and slew three thousand of their men. The aggressions of the Turks upon Egypt, ending in its conquest in 1516, gave the Mamluk Sultan of Cairo work nearer home and disabled him from further expeditions on a valid scale to the Indian coast. Almeida's victory off Diu on February 2, 1509, secured to Christendom the naval supremacy in Asia and turned the Indian Ocean for the next century into a Portuguese sea.

The first Christian Viceroy of India had done his work, but even while he was doing it King Emmanuel's views were taking a wider range. The task of Almeida was to secure the command of the Indian Ocean and he declined to divide his forces by maintaining garrisons not absolutely indispensable on shore. "The greater the number of fortresses you hold," he wrote to the king, "the weaker will be your power. Let all our forces be on the sea; because if we should not be powerful at sea (which may the Lord forbid!) everything will at once be against us." This conviction grew upon him, "now we have wars with the Venetians and Turks of the Sultan." "With the force we have at sea we will discover what these new enemies may be, for I trust in the mercy of God that He will remember us, since all the rest is of little importance. Let it be known for certain that as long as you may be powerful at sea, you will hold India as yours, and if you do not possess this power a fortress on shore will avail you little; and as to expelling the Moors (Mussulmans) from the country, I have found the right way to do it, but it is a long story, and it will be done when the Lord pleases and will thus be served."

But a sea-policy, with forts at a few dominating positions on the coast, no longer satisfied Almeida's master. King Emmanuel determined to combine the command of the Indian waters with conquest on shore. The first five years of annual expeditions from 1500 to 1505 had given the Portuguese the upper hand in the armed commerce of the Malabar coast. The following four years under Almeida, 1505–1509, left them masters of the Indian Ocean. The next six years, 1509–1515, were to see them grow under Affonso de Albuquerque into a territorial power on the Indian continent. Emmanuel the Fortunate, during his long reign from 1495 to 1521, planned and directed the whole, from the fitting forth of Vasco da Gama on his voyage of discovery to the adornment of the Portuguese capital in India with public buildings, churches, and monasteries.

Affonso de Albuquerque, on his return from his first Indian expedition in 1503–1504, had impressed his own magnificent ideas on the royal mind. In 1506 he was sent out as second in command to Tristao da Cunha with a fleet of sixteen ships to secure the mouth of the Red Sea against Egypt, while King Emmanuel despatched an-other powerful fleet to assail the Turks in the Mediterranean. The Mediterranean expedition was somewhat irrelevant; the Grand Turk at Constantinople being as little likely to aid the .rival Sultan of Egypt as Venice was honestly to help the Portuguese. But the double attack in European and Asiatic waters, if disclosing a flaw in Emmanuel's foreign intelligence attests the thoroughness of his strategy. The fleet under Da Cunha and Albuquerque, after further strengthening the Portuguese line of communication up the East African coast, took Socotra from the Mussulmans near the mouth of the Red Sea. Da Cunha then sailed to India to collect cargo, leaving Albuquerque with six ships in supreme command in the Arabian waters, in August, 1507.

Albuquerque's fixed idea was to render every capture by the Portuguese arms a permanent acquisition to the Portuguese crown. He found in Socotra a dominant population of Mussulmans and an inferior class of Asiatic Christians, corresponding in some respects to the St. Thomas Christians of Malabar. The Mussulmans he dispossessed of their lands; the old-world relics of Eastern Christianity he baptized into Catholicism, giving them, as the price of their prompt conversion, the palm-groves seized from the Mussulmans. Having built a strong fort and erected a Franciscan monastery, Albuquerque left Socotra in charge of his nephew and sailed for the Arabian coast. There, amid mutinies of his captains and troubles of many sorts, he bombarded Kuriyat and Muscat, and imposed a treaty on Ormuz designed to secure to Portugal the outlet of the Persian Gulf (1507–1508).

His plan was to cut off Ormuz from her natural supports by making himself master of the smaller harbours at the mouth of the Persian Gulf, and thus to dominate the Red Sea route from the northeast as his fortress at Socotra threatened it – from too great a distance – on the south. The mutiny of his commanders in January, 1508, arrested the complete execution of this project. But in September, 1507, the King of Ormuz had submitted to a treaty written "in letters of gold and stops blue" (the latter being doubtless the diacritical marks), acknowledging that he received "from the hand of the Captain in Chief the kingdom and seigniority of Ormuz, from which he, the Captain in Chief, had dispossessed him by force of arms," and agreeing to pay a yearly tribute to the King of Portugal with a sum down at once "to defray the men's pay which the Captain in Chief brought with him." In the autumn of 1508 Albuquerque went on to India, having vowed not to cut his beard until he built a fort at Ormuz, and leaving the king and his minister to digest these words: "Have I not already many a time told thee that I was no corsair, but Captain-General of the King of Portugal, an old man and a peaceable one?"

Middle-aged the great admiral certainly was, as he had been born in 1453; but whether peaceable, may be judged from the joint remonstrance which his captains addressed to him at Ormuz on January 5, 1508. "Sir, we do this in writing because by word of mouth we dare not, as you always answer us so passionately." Yet it was a generous fire that burned in those sunken eyes and lighted up the worn face. The ringleader of his rebellious captains, João da Nova, to whom he had been forgiving in vain, died in poverty at Cochin in 1509. "But Alfonso de Albuquerque," as his own Commentaries state, "forgot all that he had been guilty of toward himself, and only held in memory that this man had been his companion in arms and had helped him in all the troubles connected with the conquest of the kingdom of Ormuz like a cavalier, and ordered him to. be buried at his expense with the usual display of torches, and himself accompanied the body to the grave clad all in mourning." Albuquerque arrived at Cannanore in December, 1508, and produced secret orders which he carried from the king, appointing him to the supreme command in India on the expiration of the Viceroy Almeida's three years of office. He found Almeida preparing to revenge his son Lourenco slain in the gallant attempt to prevent the coalition of the Egyptian fleet with the Calicut ships. Albuquerque chivalrously acknowledged the father's claim to be himself the avenger of the noble youth, and accepted Almeida's plea that his three years of office did not expire till January, 1509. In February, 1509, Almeida, as we have seen, defeated the combined navies of Egypt and the Indian coast with terrible slaughter off Diu. But after his victorious return to Malabar he refused to give up his office, eventually threw Albuquerque into prison, and threatened to send him in chains to Lisbon. The arrival of the yearly fleet under a high officer of State, Dom Fernão de Coutinho, Marshal of Portugal, put an end to these stormy proceedings. On November 5, 1509, Almeida surrendered the supreme command to Albuquerque, and on his voyage home was killed at Saldanha Bay by the assegais of a Kaffir mob whose sheep his crew had stolen.

The six years of Albuquerque's governorship (1509–1515) raised Portugal to a territorial power in India. They are made to move before us in his own letters, and in the "Commentaries" written from his papers after his death. They were years of magnificent projects and of heroic accomplishment. To Albuquerque's far-reaching mind the struggle was not with a few port-rajas on the Malabar coast, but with the combined forces of the Mussulman world. Was the Asiatic sea-route to belong to Christendom or to Islam? Imperfectly acquainted with the conflict for Egypt between the Ottoman dynasty of Constantinople and the Mamluk Sultans of Cairo, it seemed to him, as it did to the Indian coast-princes, that the whole power of the Rumes, or Turks in the widest sense, would sooner or later be hurled against him. "The cry the Rumes are coming," he wrote, "menaced me at every step."

The magnitude of the danger explains and justifies the vastness of his designs to meet it. Some of those designs, as narrated by his biographers, belong to the region of romance. "There were two actions," writes Machado, "suggested by the magnanimity of his heart, which he determined to perform. One was to divert the channel of the Nile to the Red Sea and prevent it from running through Egypt, thereby to render the lands of the Grand Turk sterile; the other to carry away from Mecca the bones of the abominable Mafoma [Mohammed], that, these being reduced publicly to ashes, the votaries of so foul a sect might be confounded."

Apart from such grandiose conceptions, his policy was an extremely practical one, and formed a strategic whole. It consisted of three series of operations. The first series was designed to intercept the Moslem trade at its base in the Nile and Euphrates valleys, by occupying the mouths of the Persian Gulf and the Red Sea. "For it was there," he explained, "that his Highness [the King of Portugal] considered we could cut down the commerce which the Moors of Cairo, of Mecca, and of Juda carry on with these parts." This he partially accomplished by building a strong fortress at Ormuz (1515), blockading and besieging Aden, and trying to incite the Christian kingdom of Abyssinia to attack Egypt from the south. How vague was his knowledge of that semi-fabulous realm of Prester John may be inferred from Albuquerque's repeated requests for miners skilled in rock-excavation from Madeira, to tunnel a passage for the Nile through the Abyssinian mountains to the Red Sea and thus destroy the irrigation of Egypt. Partial as was his success in cutting off the Mussulman trade of Asia from its Egyptian base, his operations combined with internal disputes among the Moslems to render the cry "the Humes are coming" only a cry as long as he stood guard.

The second series of Albuquerque's operations was directed against the Mussulman trade in the Malabar ports. Those ports collected the pepper and ginger of the south Indian coast and formed emporiums for trans-shipment of the more precious spices – the cinnamon, mace, and cloves – of the farther East. Albuquerque determined not only to bring under strict control the old calling-places of the Asiatic trade-route on the Malabar littoral, but also to concentrate their commerce at a Portuguese harbour further north. He wanted a port which should command alike the trade of the southern and of the northern Bombay coast. He found what he wanted at Goa, and in 1510 he seized it. Its position, half-way between the ancient trade roadsteads in Malabar and in Gujarat, enabled the Portuguese to dominate the whole shore-line of western India from the Gulf of Cambay to Cape Comorin. The old ports of Quilon, Cochin, Cannanore, and Calicut had to submit to the restrictions placed on them in the interests of Goa. No Mussulman ship could safely trade in Malabar waters without a pass from the Christians. The conquest of Goa put the seal on Portuguese naval supremacy along the southwest Indian coast. It also involved territorial rule in India.

Albuquerque's third series of operations struck at the sources of the Mussulman trade in the Far East. The Malabar ports were merely intermediaries for the great volume of Moslem commerce which had its origin in Malacca or the Spice Archipelago and its terminus at the Egyptian ports of the Red Sea. Albuquerque resolved to cut off that commerce at its fountainhead by seizing Malacca. "For when Malacca is taken," he exhorted his captains, "the places on the Straits must be shut up, and they [the Moslems] will never more be able to introduce their spiceries into those places."

In the year 1508 King Emmanuel had despatched an expedition under Diogo Lopes de Sequeira to explore Madagascar on one side of the Indian Ocean and the Malay Peninsula on the other. Sequeira, after a friendly reception by the Sultan of Malacca, set up a factory, but underwent the usual experience of hostility from the Arab traders and treachery from the court officials. He found himself compelled to sail away, leaving the factory and twenty Portuguese at the mercy of the natives. A squadron, despatched from Lisbon in 1510 to rescue these prisoners, was retained by Albuquerque in India to assist in the capture of Goa. In 1511 Albuquerque himself undertook the task, captured Malacca, built a fortress, and established a firm Portuguese government which amid varying fortunes dominated the Malay Peninsula for a hundred years.

Albuquerque thus carried out his threefold plan by partially cutting off the Arab commerce from its western base at the mouths of the Persian Gulf and the Red Sea; by establishing a Portuguese control at Goa over the half-way marts on the Malabar coast; and by the conquest of Malacta, the most lucrative source of Moslem commerce in the Far East. The strategic design for converting the Indian Ocean from a Moslem to a Christian trade-route was complete. It only remained for his successors to fill in the details. By brilliant feats of arms and by not less skilful diplomacy they made themselves masters at dominant positions around the edge of the great Asiatic basin from the African coast to the Spice Islands. The achievement would have been a splendid one for the greatest of European powers. Accomplished by one small Christian kingdom it makes the history of Portugal read like a romance.

Albuquerque died in December, 1515, outside the Goa bar, never having been raised to the dignity of viceroy, superseded as governor, yet lifting up his hands to heaven and giving "many thanks to our Lord." "In bad repute with men because of the king," he had exclaimed when he heard of the arrival of his successor, "and in bad repute with the king because of the men, it were well that I were gone." No public statue of him exists in Lisbon, so far as I could find. Half a century elapsed after he had "finished all his troubles without seeing any satisfaction of them," before the final step was taken in the career of Portuguese supremacy which he had marked out. In 1571 the Lisbon court divided the Asiatic seas into three independent commands, with a Portuguese governor at Mozambique for the settlements on the African coast; a Portuguese viceroy at Goa for the Indian and Persian possessions; and a Portuguese governor at Malacca for the islands of the Far East.

From the time of Albuquerque the inexorable issue between Catholicism and Islam in Asia stands forth. Each side firmly believed itself fighting the battles of its God. "I trust in the passion of Jesus Christ, in whom I place all my confidence," Albuquerque declared in 1507 before entering on his governorship, "to break the spirit of the Moors." "The first ground of our policy," he wrote four years later, "is the great service which we shall perform to our Lord, in casting the Moors out of this country and quenching the fire of the sect of Mafamede [Mohammed], so that it may never burst forth again hereafter." "May God never permit," writes a Portuguese commander in 1522, "that by our neglect and sins should be lost what has cost so much of the martyrs' blood." The most precious gift brought to Goa by an ambassador, real or pretended, from Abyssinia was "the wood of the Holy True Cross," according to a letter of Duarte Barbosa for the king, dated January 12, 1513, and preserved in the India Office

Mss. The Moslems, appealing with equal confidence to Allah, called the Faithful to the sacred war. "We desire nought else but to be close to God," runs their summons in 1539. It denounces the aggressions "of the Christians of Portugal," and warns an Indian prince that, if he holds back, his "soul will descend into hell."

To "the martyrs' blood" of the Portuguese and the relic of the Blessed Rood from Abyssinia, the Moslems oppose their "Holy Fleet." First the Arabs of the Indian ports supply "the fighters for the faith." Then the Mamluk Sultan of Cairo sends armaments. Finally enters on the scene the mighty power of the Turkish empire, which deemed its subjugation of Egypt incomplete as long as the Portuguese threatened the Red Sea. The Arabs of the Indian ports quickly succumbed to the cavaliers of the Cross. The Mamluk Sultans of Egypt, hard pushed by the Ottomans from the north, could make no headway against the Portuguese in the east. But the Turks, or "Rumes," turned back the tide of Christian conquest in Asia.

The cry "the Rumes are coming," which afflicted Albuquerque, forever resounded in the ears of his successors. When the Portuguese closed the Malabar shore route to the Moslem world, the Arab ships struck boldly across the Indian Ocean from Aden to south of Ceylon, passing through the Maldive Islands or far out at sea. When the Portuguese secured the strong position of Diu at the north entrance to Indian waters, the Turks constantly harassed that station and tried to outflank it by menacing the Portuguese factories westwards on the Persian Gulf. When the Portuguese sought the enemy in the Red Sea, they were often repulsed, and their momentary successes at Aden ended in lasting failure. In vain the Lisbon court tried to make a few years' arrangement with the Turks, offering in 1541 to supply pepper in exchange for wheat, and passes for Moslem ships in Indian waters in return for free entrance of Portuguese ships to Aden and the Arabian ports of the Red Sea.

The unholy project came to nought. Four years later, in 1545, the Turks boldly attacked the Portuguese Diu; in 1547, their janizaries appeared before Portuguese Malacca; in 1551 and again in 1581 their galleys sacked Portuguese Muscat. In the next chapter we shall see a rough demarcation arrived at between the Portuguese and Turkish spheres of influence on the Persian coast – but a line ever shifting with the fortunes of a ceaseless war. After the union of the two Iberian crowns in 1580, as before it, the Portuguese in Asia remained the outflanking force of Christendom against the Turk.

They not only drained the Ottoman resources by intercepting the flow of wealth from India to Egypt and Constantinople. They also compelled a diversion of the Turkish fighting power from the Mediterranean to the Red Sea. The "martyrs' blood" of the Portuguese, poured forth during a century on the Indian Ocean, was a constant factor in the conflict between the Holy Roman Empire and the Ottomans in Europe – that long grapple between Christianity and Islam fought out on the line of the Danube and summed up by the sea-fight of Lepanto (1571).

The story of Portugal's work in Asia will, I trust, be one day told to the English-speaking world in a manner worthy of the theme. For such a history ample materials, printed and manuscript, are now available. My present object is merely to bring into view the struggle between Islam and Christendom for the Indian Ocean in the century preceding the appearance of the English on the scene. I dare not expand these preliminary chapters by the deeds of heroism and chivalrous devotion on both sides. Nor is it permitted to me to attempt even the most rapid sketch of the separate expeditions, with their skilful combination of sea and land power, which secured the triumph of Portugal on the Indian coast-line. I have had to mention the successive armaments sent forth during the years following Da Gama's discovery, for almost each of them marked a stage in the swift development of the Portuguese power in the East. But the long rule of Affonso Albuquerque gave fixity to the programme. It becomes possible, therefore, to pass over subsequent operations, however important they may be in themselves, and to trace the main lines of the policy by which his great design was accomplished.

Chapter 4 – The Portuguese Policy in the East

1500–1600

The actual achievement of Portugal in Asia was not a land-empire, but the overlordship of the sea. Her sphere of influence stretched eastwards across the vast basin six thousand miles from the African coast to the Moluccas, and northward four thousand miles from the Cape of Good Hope to the Persian Gulf. Her political frontier, that is the line which she had more or less continuously to hold, was not defended by rivers or mountains. It was the open edge of the ocean following, at the height of the Portuguese power, a sinuous route from Natal northeast to Ormuz, from Ormuz southeast to Cape Comorin, from Comorin northeast again to Bengal, then southeast to Malacca, Java, and the Spice Islands – a jagged semicircle of over fifteen thousand miles. That a small European nation, then numbering perhaps not more than a million of souls, should continue to hold this frontier was impossible when stronger European rivals came upon the scene. That Portugal should have held it for a century against the Mussulman world is an enduring glory to herself and to Christendom.

How to make the most of her slender resources in this stupendous task was, from the arrival of her first viceroy, Almeida, the supreme problem of Portugal in India Almeida (1505–1509) believed, as we have seen, that the solution lay in an exclusively sea policy, supported by as few forts as possible at dominant positions on the Indian coast. Albuquerque took a wider view. He realized that the command of the sea, separated by a fourth of the globe from his European base, must depend upon a line of shore supports whence he could draw both revenues and supplies. "My will and determination is, as long as I am governor," runs his famous speech to his captains at Malacca in 1511, "neither to fight nor to hazard men on land, except in those parts wherein I must build a fortress to maintain them."

"If it be the wish of our Lord," he wrote to the king in 1512, "to dispose the commerce of India in such a manner that the goods and wealth contained in her should be forwarded to you year by year in your squadrons, I do not believe that in all Christendom there will be so rich a king as your Highness. And therefore do I urge you, Senhor, to work up warmly this affair of India with men and arms and strengthen your hold in her and securely establish your dealings and your factories. And that you wrest the wealth of India and business from the hands of the Moors, and this by good fortresses gaining the principal places of business of the Moors." The Moslem opposition "will subsist in India so long as they do not see in your power the principal forces of the country, and good strongholds or a power of men to keep them at peace." Albuquerque thus sums up his demand – either a great fleet and an army, or the seizure and fortification of the principal towns "on the shores of the sea."

Again in 1513, as regards attacks from the Rumes, or Turkish Empire, "I hold it to be free from doubt that if fortresses be built in Diu and Calicut (as I trust in our Lord they will be), when once they have been well fortified, if a thousand of the Sultan's ships were to make their way to India, not one of those places could be brought again under his dominion." "I would strongly point out," he had written to King Emmanuel in 1510, "the uselessness of sending any more ships to these waters, as the supply of vessels here is ample. What we require is a large supply of arms, ammunition, and materials of war."

In carrying out this policy, says Machado, "he erected with an expense equal to their magnificence the fortresses of Malacca, Ormuz, Calicut, Cochin, and Cannanore, inscribed on whose stones his name is handed down to posterity under the glorious title of Founder of the Portuguese Empire in the East."

Albuquerque's plan of seizing strongholds, wherever convenient on the coast, might easily degenerate into a system of piratical descents. As a matter of fact, Goa, by far the largest acquisition of the Portuguese in India, was captured with the aid of a famous corsair, Timoja, during the absence of its lawful prince. But however we may stigmatize such attacks, they merely extended to Asia the state of war then chronic between Christendom and Islam in Europe. The Papal Bulls seemed to the sixteenth century the literal fulfilment of the Scriptural promise and command: "Ask of me, and I shall give thee the heathen for thine inheritance, and the uttermost parts of the earth for thy possession. Thou shalt break them with a rod of iron; thou shalt dash them in pieces like a potter's vessel." The Portuguese historian De Barros denied to unbelievers the international rights pertaining to states within the comity of Christendom. A similar sentiment may be cited from our own Coke, and although Coke's view was afterward condemned by Lord Mansfield, it is not the less representative of the age to which it belonged.

The Holy See distinguished, indeed, between negative unbelievers who had never heard of the faith, and positive unbelievers who, having knowledge of the faith, received it not, or subsequently renounced it, and, in judging the Inquisition, we should not forget that it seemed at first a defence of Christian Spain against Islam. King Emmanuel of Portugal met the difficulty from the outset, by embarking in 1500 A.D. a band of friars as mentioned in the preceding chapter, with his expedition of 1200 fighting men, and instructing Cabral as follows: "Before he attacked the Moors and idol-aters of those parts with the material and secular sword, he was to allow the priests and monks to use their spiritual sword which was to declare to them the Gospel ... and convert them to the faith of Christ. ... And should they be so contumacious as not to accept this law of faith ... and should they forbid commerce and exchange ... in that case they should put them to fire and sword, and carry on fierce war against them." The Portuguese king thus regularized his position from the theological point of view. The same sentiment of no common faith, no common rights, still influences the European attitude toward the African races; but for the words Christianity and paganism we now use the terms civilization and barbarism.

In carrying out the doctrine of lawful war against all unbelievers, with whom no express compact existed to the contrary, the Portuguese were led into cruelties, in part common to that time, but in part arising from their peculiar position in Asia. Their force was so small that they thought it needful to punish without mercy any resistance or revolt. This necessity for terrorizing the superior numbers of their enemies may explain, though it can never excuse, the atrocities which stained their history in the East. Such severities became a fixed principle of their policy from the second voyage of Vasco da Gama in 1502. The Bishop Osorio blames Almeida (1505–1509) for torturing and executing the prisoners after the battle of Diu, and reprobates the conduct of a captain who in 1507 threw the crew of an Arab ship sewed up in sails into the sea, although they had not defended themselves and held a Portuguese passport. Almeida "blew his prisoners from guns before Cannanore, saluting the town with their fragments." On the capture of Brava, the Portuguese soldiers "barbarously cut off the hands and ears of women, to take off their bracelets and earrings, to save time in taking them off."

These were not exceptional barbarities. The permanent attitude of the Portuguese to all Asiatics who resisted was void of compunction.

To quote a few examples from contemporary manuscripts: a letter from João de Lima to the King of Portugal in 1518 speaks of the people of Daibul as "dogs" who "do not want but the sword in hand." In 1535, at the capture of the petty island of Mete near Diu, "all were killed, without allowing a single one to live, and for this reason it was henceforward called the Island of the Dead." In 1540 the Zamorin was compelled to agree to cast out of his dominions all who would not accept the terms imposed, "and if they should not wish to go, he will order them to be killed." In 1546, says the official report of the siege of Diu, "we spared no life whether of women or children."

I cut short the list of horrors. The Portuguese cruelties were deliberate rather than vindictive. Even a high-minded soldier and devout cavalier of the Cross like Albuquerque believed a reign of terror to be a necessity of his position, and that, in giving no quarter, he best rendered service to Christ and acted with the truest humanity in the long run to the heathen. So inherently noble was he felt to be, that in after years both Hindus and Mohammedans were wont to repair to his tomb, and there, as in the presence of his shade, to call upon God to deliver them from the tyranny of his successors. Yet even his lofty soul stooped to the atrocities of cutting off the ears and noses of his prisoners, of hunting in rowboats after despairing wretches who had thrown themselves overboard and hacking them to pieces in the water, and of slaying the women and children of captured. towns. Terrorism had to take the place of strength. It was a device to which the Portuguese were compelled by plans of conquest beyond their national resources.

The main object of the Portuguese in Asia was a monopoly of the Indo-European trade. I propose, without dwelling on individual feats of arms, to show briefly how that monopoly was secured, partly by treaties and partly by war; how it was maintained by a combined naval and military force; what the monopoly consisted of, and the mercantile methods by which it was worked.

The more important treaties of Portugal in the East followed a common type, and Albuquerque's first agreement with Ormuz may be taken as an illustration of the whole. In that instrument the "King of Ormuz" (1) acknowledges himself a vassal to the Portuguese sovereign, (2) grants a site for a factory and fortress, (3) submits to a yearly tribute and agrees to a payment toward the expenses of the troops which had coerced him. These three main heads of political dependence, a fortified factory, and a tribute or money payment, supplied the model for subsequent treaties, wherever the Portuguese found themselves strong enough to enforce them. They were the standard of subjection which the Portuguese sought to impose on the coast-powers from the Red Sea to the Moluccas. The system developed into an endeavour to exempt Portuguese vessels from dues at the Indian ports and to extract a revenue for Portugal from the local customs tariff. But the length of the coast-line to be coerced, and the unequal forces employed for the task, render generalizations unsafe. The treaty-history of Portugal in the East may be best understood. from some characteristic examples.

Calicut, being defiant and one of the strongest positions on the Indian coast, for a time treated on advantageous terms. The compact of 1513 provided for the exchange of pepper and ginger at fair rates for the Portuguese imports, allowed the Calicut Zamorin to send two trading-ships under Portuguese passes to Ormuz during the current year, and agreed that Portuguese merchandise should pay dues. A fortified factory was then built and the bond was soon drawn tighter.

By the treaty of 1515 the Zamorin of Calicut expresses a desire to serve Portugal; will allow no enemies of Portugal to enter his harbour; gives exemptions to Christians, even to Christian converts; and is to pay half the shipping-dues to the Portuguese. The process of coercion went on till in 1540 the Calicut Zamorin agreed to sell "all the pepper" and "all the ginger there may be on his lands to the King our Lord," to harbour no enemies of Portugal nor to make war on its friends, to give up his trade with the Arabian coast, to allow none of his subjects to sail thither, and to keep no war-vessels or even armed rowboats. By this time Calicut, her chief, and her commerce were in the grip of the Portuguese fort.

Other towns on the Indian seaboard must be dealt with more briefly. The Portuguese in their struggle with Calicut entered into engagements with rival coast-chiefs which they could not always fulfil. In 1500–1501 Cabral, having signed a treaty with the friendly Cochin raja, promised some day to make him Zamorin of Calicut. After wars and distresses suffered by the little State in the Portuguese cause, the Cochin raja thus pours out his sorrows in a letter to King Emmanuel in 1513." Your Highness sent me a golden crown, as a sign that I was crowned the chief king of the whole of India. ... And your governor especially crowned me as king, and he declared on oath that he would make me the chief king of all India, and assist me against anyone who should come upon me And I also promised to assist him against whoever should come upon them and to stand to the defence of your fortress until death, and in this manner they swore to it by oath in the church." Yet after twelve years these fine promises remained empty words, and here was Albuquerque in 1513 making treaties with Calicut to the detriment of Cochin.

Quilon, with its Portuguese factory and fort since 1503, being still weaker than Cochin, fared worse. Certain disturbances having taken place at Quilon during the absence of the queen, the church of the old St. Thomas Christians is in 1516 to be rebuilt, according to the terms of a treaty dated September 25, 1516, and the Christians favoured as formerly, and treated "even better, if that can be." It was further agreed, four years later, that if any native "whether Gentile or Moor or any other description whatever should wish to become a Christian, that he be free to do so without any one preventing him, or any obstacle offered whatever." The death of the Portuguese factor at Quilon, for which the disclaimers of guilt by the queen and her chiefs were accepted, was punished by a fine of two hundred thousand pounds of pepper. By the treaty of 1520 the St. Thomas Christians were further protected, and received a site under the guns of the Portuguese fortress; the monopoly of all pepper grown in Quilon was secured to the Portuguese king; and all Portuguese ships were to pay their dues to him. Finally, in 1548, it was conceded that the Portuguese were to be exempt from dues "in the quays of the sea, where the embarkation takes place for Cochin."

The Portuguese hold on the Persian Gulf was in like manner tightened. In 1515 Albuquerque completed the fortress at Ormuz. By the treaty of 1523, the Portuguese are to pay no dues at Ormuz except on exports, and the whole kingdom of Ormuz is to be delivered up on demand to the King of Portugal. Meanwhile in each year Ormuz shall pay in lieu of giving over the custom house, "in tributes and vassalage to the King our Lord in silver, gold, and seed pearls, to the value of the land sixty thousand xerafins." All Christian renegades are to be handed over to the captain of the Portuguese fortress, and no Moslems shall carry arms in Ormuz save the attendants on the king and town magistrate. Any other Moor wearing arms "shall on the second offence be flogged, and on the third be put to death." Moslems are to pay duty on all merchandise, Portuguese are to be exempt. The Moslems are to maintain a chief of police who should be a Christian and "twenty Christian men who walked with him." Six years later a heavy fine was laid on Orrauz for the death of the Portuguese magistrate, and the customs revenue was allotted until payment should be realized. In 1540 a custom house and certain revenues were formally made over to the Portuguese, subject to allowances to the Ormuz court – "in payment of tributes," says the King of Ormuz not without pathos, "which I am obliged to pay."

While the entrance to the Persian Gulf thus passed completely under the Portuguese, it also marked the western limits of their shore-power on the Indo-Egyptian route. Their attempts to seize the mouth of the Red Sea failed. In 1513 Albuquerque, after a bloody siege of Aden, was repulsed with slaughter, and could only cannonade the tow-n and burn the ships in the harbour. The brave Arabs had no intention of yielding their stronghold, from which they could swoop down on the Red Sea passage, to Christian, Egyptian, or Turk. In 1516 the Sultan of Cairo failed, as Albuquerque had failed, to capture Aden. Soon after there came an overwhelming fleet of forty Portuguese ships and three thousand soldiers, and the battered fortress offered to surrender. But the fleet sailed on to attack the Moslem navy in the Red Sea, and by the time it got back to Aden the defences were repaired and the offer was withdrawn. The Turks, when they wrested Egypt from the Mamluk Sultans in 1517, perceived that Aden was necessary to complete their conquest. During the struggle which followed, the Aden ruler submitted at moments to the Portuguese. In 1524 and again in 1530 he "rendered himself a vassal to Dom João of Portugal" and agreed to pay a yearly tribute, with the gift of "a crown of gold" as first-fruits to his Majesty.

Such submissions, however, were merely Arab merely feints to gain a breathing-space. In 1538 Solyman the Magnificent closed the struggle by an expedition which captured Aden. But even the forces of the Ottoman empire at its zenith only won the place by stratagem. The Turkish sailors were carried ashore on beds pleading for the hospitality which Mussulmans everywhere show to the sick of their religion. The ruler of Aden received them generously, was gratefully invited on board the Turkish fleet, and then treacherously hanged. For a time Solyman the Magnificent dominated the whole Arabian coast from Aden, strengthened by one hundred guns and a garrison of five hundred Turks. But before the middle of the century the Arab population rose and handed over the fort in despair to the Portuguese. Aden was finally retaken by the Pasha of Egypt in 1551, and remained amid varying fortunes a Turkish outpost until 1630, when it passed again to the Arabs of the Yemen province. From Albuquerque's attack in 1513 on, it stood defiant just outside the limits of the Indo-Portuguese power.

While Aden thus prevented the complete execution of Albuquerque's scheme for cutting off the Moslem trade from its Egyptian base, his designs on the sources of that trade in the Far East were more fully carried out. The cheaper spices of the Indian coast, pepper and ginger, he secured by his command of the Malabar ports. The Moslem monopoly of the cinnamon of Ceylon and of the precious cloves and mace of the Archipelago, was broken by Albuquerque's seizure of Malacca (1511), with subsequent captures and treaties by his successors. My business, however, is with India, and I dare not follow the brilliant track of Portuguese achievement in eastern Asia. The Moluccas, or Spice Islands, the richest jewels in the Portuguese crown when formally made over by Spain in 1529, became not only a source of trade but of tribute; Tidore, for example, paying in cloves. In 1564 the king of the Moluccas yielded to Portugal the dominion and lordship of the whole of his territories.

The Portuguese sovereign, indeed, gave full powers to his captain in Malacca "to take possession or part possession, as the case may be, of any lands, places, and islands" which that officer or his subordinates should "discover or arrive at," and "to acquire in my name the lordship of the said places, lands, and islands," as stated in the preamble to the treaty with the Island of Sunda, dated January 27, 1532. Under these powers the royal arms of Portugal were fixed up on many a remote shore, a flag with the cross of Christ being handed to the inhabitants and a green bough delivered by way of ratification.

"Having come to the island Amene" (a poor little islet a mile and a half in diameter in the Laccadives), runs one treaty, signed February 4, 1560, which may serve as an example of how the system practically worked, the Portuguese commodore "went on land and destroyed it and slew many people and took a great number, and coming to a convention of peace" – it was agreed that the rulers should make over the group of islands to the King of Portugal and pay a tribute of cocoanut fibre, with the pledge of a green branch "in sign of peace and obedience," "for as much as they did not wish to be vassals of any other king or lord."

If this was Portugal's short way with the naked islanders of the Laccadives, she had an ascending scale of refinement in dealing with the more powerful rajas of the Indian coast and Eastern Archipelago. The treaties leave more or less to the native rulers the jurisdiction over their own. subjects. While insisting strongly on the privileges of native Christians, and placing them under the jurisdiction of the Portuguese fort, they generally respect the rights of the professors of other faiths. The treaty with the warlike King of Gujarat, in 1534, guaranteed the revenues of the Bassein mosques, "and what preaching should take place in them," from "any innovation whatever." In the Moluccas the viceroy agreed, in 1539, that "no Portuguese should enter into the mosques of the Moors; and on his entering and doing evil things, he shall be apprehended by the Moors or by the Christians and delivered up at the fortress, for me to punish according to his fault. Forasmuch as I think it to the service of the King my Lord that the mosques be guarded against the Portuguese and be as honoured as are our own churches." In at least one case, according to a contract with the King of Gujarat, October 25, 1535, conversions were forbidden on either side, but were often provided for on the side of the Christians. Some protection was even attempted for the pagodas or temples of the Hindus, as is shown by a contract with Mealecao Malik Khan), dated April 24, 1555; and the contract of 1520 provided against the killing of cows in the Quilon State.

I have dwelt on the treaty-aspects of the Portuguese policy in the East, not merely because they illustrate the actual dealings of Portugal with Asiatic states, but because such engagements became in the next century a factor in European diplomacy. One of the initial difficulties which the English East India Company had to face was the Portuguese claim that the princes of the Indian coast and Spice Archipelago were, under these treaties, subjects of the Portuguese crown, and that their territories formed part of the Portuguese dominions.

The Portuguese clearly understood that their power depended on their fleet, and showed a wise jealousy of sea rivals. But the shipbuilding of the Atlantic so greatly excelled that of the Indian Ocean, that only two states of Western India could seriously imperil the Christian squadrons. The navies of Calicut and Gujarat, aided by the Egyptian admiral, had matched themselves against the Viceroy Almeida, and their defeat at Diu was followed up by treaties to prevent their reconstruction. Calicut in the south was not allowed to keep war-vessels or even armed rowing-boats. Gujarat on the north had, in 1534, to agree that no warship should be built in any of her ports, a condition reinforced by subsequent treaties. The same unsparing policy which flogged and sentenced to death the Arabs of Ormuz who ventured to carry arms, also put an end to naval construction at alien Indian harbours.

Portugal further coerced the naval states of Western India by a chain of settlements at strategic points up the coast. Besides the fortress factories already mentioned on the southern Malabar seaboard, the four important positions of Goa, Bassein close to Bombay, Daman on the Gujarat shore, and Diu at the point of the Kathiawar peninsula, were turned by conquest or treaty into Portuguese strongholds. The island fortress of Diu commanded the approach to India from the Persian Gulf just where ships rounded into the Gulf of Cambay, and formed a bulwark against the Arab, Egyptian, or Turkish line of attack. Its conquest and retention cost the Portuguese more blood and treasure than any other of their Indian possessions.

Goa, their principal settlement, dominated the south Indian ports, as Diu controlled the coast-route on the north. The pirate chief Timoja proposed to Albuquerque that as the lord of Goa was dead (in reality absent) they should seize the place. This they easily did in March, 1510. But the rightful sovereign, a son of the Ottoman Sultan Amurad II, whose romantic adventures had ended with his carving for himself the kingdom of Bijapur in southern India, hurried back to Goa and drove out the Portuguese in May. During three months of terrible sufferings and heroic endurance, the Portuguese were wind-bound in the estuary within the Goa bar and exposed to a superior force on shore. But eventually they got to sea, and when the king was again called away by disturbances in the interior, they recaptured Goa with the help of the pirate Timoja in November, 1510. Its rightful sovereign, Yusuf Adil Shah, the king of Bijapur, died in the following month (December 5th). His son was a minor, and during the first years of his reign it was all his ministers could do to hold together the most important inland provinces of the Bijapur kingdom. The outlying island of Goa and its region of creeks and estuaries remained with the Portuguese.

The pirate Timoja, who first urged Albuquerque to seize it, and whose forces bore an important part in its capture and recapture, received a substantial share of the spoils. He obtained the revenues of a district in free gift, was appointed chief Aguazil, or administrator, of the lands of Goa, and captain of the native population. The revenues of the whole annexed territories, Goa Island excepted, were made over to him in return for a fixed rental, together with the responsibility for their defence. That daring and unscrupulous corsair was exactly the sort of adventurer then founding dynasties in India. Had he lived he might have set up a coast kingdom of his own and proved a troublesome neighbour to the Portuguese. But here again fortune favoured the Christians. This Timoja enjoyed his new accession of power only for a year, and died in 1511.

As Diu was the Portuguese outpost which controlled the passage into Indian waters on the north, so Goa became their central place of arms and commerce half-way down the coast. Its nucleus, the Island of Goa proper, was defended by rivers or creeks on both sides from the mainland, and by capes on the north and south from the extreme fury of the monsoons. The silting of the channels which now impedes the approach was then in an earlier stage, and the Goa anchorage, with twenty-one feet at high water and eighteen at low, sufficed for the largest shipping of that time. In 1641–1648 Tavernier regarded it as one of the best harbours in the world. It was, in fact, an earlier Bombay, guarded yet not cut off from the mainland by marine backwaters or river-arms, and nearer than Bombay to the ancient ports of Indo-European commerce. Al-though Goa Island was but nine miles long by three broad, the trade of the western coast was gradually concentrated at its quays. Its natural advantages were developed by a skilful system of treaty restrictions and exemptions at the expense of the old Malabar ports; and even the silting up of the channels was for a time overcome by moving the town nearer to the sea.

The old Goa which Albuquerque captured is now a city of empty convents and monasteries; mounds of broken bricks, once palaces, buried under rank grass; and streets overgrown with cocoanut-trees and jungle. The churches rise mournfully amid the desolation. "Il ne reste plus de cette ville que le sacré," said the superior of the Augustinian convent in 1827: "le profane en est entierement banni." "The river washes the remains of a great city," wrote Sir William Howard Russell fifty years later, in 1877, "an arsenal in ruins, palaces in ruins, quay walls in ruins – all in ruins." The still older Goa, built by the native kings, I could only trace by little square rice-fields which marked the ground plan of fortress courts and palace quadrangles. Panjim and New Goa, which became the residence of the viceroy in 1759, are threatened with a like deterioration. But a railway, built by British enterprise, now connects Marmagao with the southern Maratha line, and holds out hopes of a return to commercial importance.

Yet before its decay, Goa had a carnival of prosperity which proves what a commercial war-policy can for a time effect. "Goa Dourado," or Golden Goa, was a place of fabulous wealth to the plain London merchants who were struggling into an East India Company under Elizabeth. "Whoever hath seen Goa need not see Lisbon," ran the Portuguese proverb. The accounts of the city given by Linschoten, Pyrard de Laval, Fitch, Della Valle, and other European travellers who visited Goa in the sixteenth or early in the seventeenth century show that it combined the riches of commerce with the splendours of ecclesiastical pomp and a powerful military court. The work of the community was done by slaves, whose toil chiefly supplied the in-comes of the Portuguese inhabitants; for in Goa no Portuguese of decent birth could follow a trade without disgrace, nor could his wife busy herself in domestic labours without losing her social position. The only respectable livelihoods were the Church, the army, and government employ – with buccaneering and seagoing commerce in a few vigorous hands.

The intensely military spirit, and its contempt for peaceful industry, ended in a reaction of profligacy and sloth. Portuguese society in Goa divided itself into two idle populations – an idle population of men in the streets and gaming-saloons, and an idle population of women in the seclusion of their own homes. The gambling-houses, sumptuously furnished and paying a heavy license-tax to the Government, were the resort of dancing girls, jugglers, native actors, and buffoons – haunts of iniquity, in which the more determined players stayed sometimes for days together and were provided with board and lodging. The ladies of Goa soon obtained an equally unenviable name. Shut up as much as possible from male society, they lounged half-dressed through the tropical day, singing, playing, quarrelling, gossiping with their flattering slaves, "and especially devising means to elude the vigilance of their husbands." Such is the statement of Da Fonseca on the authority of Linschoten and Pyrard in the sixteenth century. A European zantina life grew up and produced ugly consequences. A lady valued herself in her female coterie upon the number and daring of her intrigues. The travellers who visited Goa during its prime tell strange tales of the hardihood with which the Portuguese mashtrons pursued their amours – not scrupling to stupefy the husband with drugs, and then admitting the paramour to his chamber. The perils of such interviews gave zest to jaded appetite, and the Goanese became a byword as the type of an Orientalized community, idle, haughty, and corrupt.

But the Portuguese of Goa, although clad much like natives in their own houses, save for the large rosaries round their necks, and with their children running "up and down the house naked till they begin to be old enough to be ashamed," made a splendid appearance when they stirred abroad. The ladies in gorgeous apparel were carried in not less gorgeous litters, guarded by domestics, to the great functions of the Church – their "dress mostly of gold and silver brocade adorned with pearls, precious stones, and with jewels on the head, arms, hands, and round the waist; and they put on a veil of the finest crepe in the world, which extends from head to foot." They wore no stockings, but slippers studded with gems, and raised on cork soles nearly half a foot in height." "They do not wear any mask, but paint their cheeks to a shameful degree." "These ladies, when they enter the church, are taken by the hand by one or two men, since they cannot walk by themselves on account of the height of the slippers." Each is thus helped "to her seat some forty or fifty paces off, taking at least a good quarter of an hour to walk that distance, so slowly and majestically does she move" – after the fashion of the high-born Venetian ladies of that time. For these and the following statements we may look again to Pyrard and other early authorities.

When a gentleman rode forth he was attended by a throng of slaves in gay and fanciful liveries, some holding painted umbrellas, others displaying richly inlaid arms; while his horse glittered with gold and silver trappings, jingling silver bells, reins studded with precious stones, and gilt stirrups wrought into artistic patterns. The poor aped the rich and resorted to amusing makeshifts to exhibit an air of grandeur. Gentlemen who lived together had a few silk suits between them in common. "These they used by turns when they went out, and hired the services of a man to hold an umbrella over them as they strutted through the streets."

As Goa declined, its pride and poverty increased. Tavernier (1648) relates how once wealthy families were reduced to seeking alms, yet they did not put aside their vanity. The Portuguese matrons, like the Roman lady in Juvenal, went forth on their round of beggary in palanquins, attended by servants who delivered their petitions to those whose charity they implored.

I have dwelt on the interior life of Goa, for it represented, on a more magnificent scale, the social types and standards of the other Portuguese settlements in India. The European force by which those settlements were maintained was a comparatively small one; probably never exceeding eight thousand men; although I have failed to obtain conclusive evidence on this point. For the projected expedition against Diu in 1522, on which the Portuguese desired to concentrate their whole power, six thousand men were requested. In 1524 the king was bluntly told that "if your Highness had in India four thousand of such men as "a certain captain," they would perform greater feats than what is now done by the seven thousand or eight thousand who are walking about here." In 1535 the viceroy in Goa prepared to meet the great Turkish armament with seven thousand men and 120 ships. These numbers refer to supreme efforts of Portugal in the East, and they were only in part made up of Europeans. Albuquerque's plan submitted to the king in 1512 involved a force of three thousand men for three years. Manuscript letters in the India Office are our authority for the various statements here made.

The practice of enlisting native soldiers commenced with the first foothold obtained by the Portuguese in India. In 1504 Pacheco defended Cochin with a garrison of three hundred Malabar soldiers and one hundred to one hundred and fifty Portuguese – besides the levies under the native king. Albuquerque employed two hundred native soldiers in taking Goa (1510), and one thousand of them at a single position during its subsequent defence. His Indian troops consisted partly of Nairs, partly of the ancient native Christians of Malabar, and it was a native Christian soldier who first forced his way through the arsenal door into the city. After its final recapture, Albuquerque advanced with a mixed force of one thousand Portuguese and two thousand native troops. How far the native soldiers in these early operations were drilled, it is difficult to say, but the contemporary records disclose bodies of Asiatics as a regular part of the trained Portuguese forces, both on shore and in distant sea expeditions. To quote only a few examples: Albuquerque employed a mixed force of 1700 Portuguese and 830 Indians against Aden in 1513; and 1500 Portuguese with 700 Indians against Ormuz in 1515; while Soarez in 1516 sailed for the Red Sea with 1200 Portuguese, 800 Indian soldiers, and 800 Indian seamen.

The last instance exhibits a high proportion of natives for that early period, but the Portuguese employed Asiatic troops in increasing numbers. The cavalry remained for the most part European; the infantry consisted largely if not chiefly of Indians. In 1520 the commandant of Goa seized part of the adjacent mainland with 250 horse and eight hundred Canarese foot-soldiers. Even in the distant Archipelago, the attacking force at Bantam in 1525 was made up of six hundred Portuguese and four hundred Malays.

As the slave population increased in the Portuguese settlements by capture, purchase, and traffic, it was employed in military service. Human beings were cheap in India in those times of wars, raids, and famines: a slave was valued in Bengal at fourteen shillings, "and a young woman of good appearance at about as much again." For the great expedition against Aden in 1530 Nuno da Cunha got together a fleet of four hundred vessels, most of them small craft fitted out by natives, with a force of 3600 Portuguese soldiers, 1460 Portuguese sailors, 2000 Indian soldiers, 5000 Indian seamen, and 8000 slaves. In 1542 Fort Sangaga was relieved by a force of 160 Portuguese, 20 horse, and 2000 natives. In 1567 the Malacca garrison consisted of 1500 men, of whom only 200 were Portuguese. In 1570 a thou-sand slaves were joined to the regular troops for the defence of Goa.

The truth is that the Portuguese settler soon became an unmanageable and a reluctant foot-soldier. Albuquerque, following the example of Alexander the Great in his Asiatic conquests, and of Hamilcar in Spain, encouraged his troops to marry native wives. The Lisbon court supplied dowries for these unions which at once created the nucleus of a female Catholic population and yearly added infants to the Faith. It soon appeared, however, that such nuptials had another aspect. In 1513 Duarte Barbosa raised his voice against

paying more for marriages to men who afterwards became Moors, than the worth of what Goa has produced up to the present, or ever will produce." But the priests defended the system, the Government provided posts for the husbands, and the records show a frequent desire that "the married people "should be greatly favoured. A languid population of half-breeds sprang up, and employment had to be found for them. In 1569 the attacking force on Parnel included 100 Portuguese, 50 Moorish horse, and 650 half-caste soldiers. Three years previously, in 1566, a militia, chiefly natives and half-breeds, had been organized for Goa – divided in 1630 into a body of regulars 2500 strong, and a defensive reserve of 5000 men.

As the flow of pay from the treasury dried up, the Portuguese soldiers and their half-caste descendants degenerated into a military mob, selling their muskets to native princes and stooping to every disgrace to fill their stomachs. In 1548 the King of Portugal was implored to allow war-service grants to the soldiers, "for they walk day and night at the doors, begging for the love of God. And if it would but end here it would be a lesser evil. But they go over to the Moors because they give them wages and allow them to live at their own liberty." What stipends they received they gambled away.

The native infantry were disciplined and directed by Portuguese officers, but sometimes led by their own. Antonio Fernandes Chale, for example, a Malabar native Christian, held important command under Portuguese generals, and was raised to the dignity of a Knight of the military Order of Christ. Slain in action in 1571, he received a state funeral at Goa. In the previous year, 1570, the viceroy manned the defensive works of Goa against Adil Khan . with 1500 native troops under Portuguese officers, holding his little force of seven hundred Portuguese as a reserve to support whatever position might be hardest pressed. "I certify to your Highness," wrote Pedro de Faria to the king as early as 1522 about the Calicut troops, "that they are as good as ours" and are practised in shooting three times a week. The differences in drill and weapons were not so decisively in favour of the European system in the sixteenth century as they afterwards became:

The chivalrous confidence of the first Portuguese adventurers in their Christian saints degenerated among their half-caste successors into a vague hope of supernatural succour, a habit' of "always awaiting the benefits of our Lord working miracles on our behalf – which is a trying thing."

I have confined my survey to the period preceding the union of Portugal with the Spanish crown in 1580. After that event the necessities of Spain in Europe did not give the Portuguese a fair chance in India. But even before it, the resources of Portugal were being exhausted. The African slave-trade which had supplied forced labour for the tillage of Portugal and set free the coast peasantry especially in the south for enterprise beyond the seas, had eaten like a canker into the nation. In the sixteenth century whole districts of Portugal were partitioned into great estates cultivated by slaves and denuded of their free population, who flocked to the capital. The Portuguese in India in like manner depended more and more for their subsistence on slave labour, and for their defence on Indian troops. The officers of the Indian Department at Lisbon and at Goa embezzled pay for seventeen thousand soldiers, while only four thousand were actually kept up. The native troops became masters of the situation. After many troubles they had to be disbanded, and, when re-established on a different footing, commenced in our own day a fresh course of mutiny and revolt.

That Portugal succeeded even for a time in imposing her supremacy on the Asiatic trade-route was due to her fleet. Between 1497 and 1612 no fewer than 806 ships were employed in the Indian trade; of which 425 returned to Europe, 285 remained permanently on the Asiatic stations, and ninety-six were lost. Their ordinary size varied from 100 to 550 tons, armed with cannon and fitted out for purposes both of freight and war. The ambition of the naval constructors of Portugal outran their technical skill and ended in floating castles which could not stand the Indian voyage. Twenty-two of these unseaworthy monsters were lost between 1579 and 1591, partly due to overlading and partly to their unwieldy size. The Madre de Deos, a huge erection with "three close decks, seven stories, a main orlop, a forecastle, and a spar deck of two floors," measured 165 feet from beak to stern, and nearly forty-seven feet across the second "close deck." Besides the ships from Europe, vessels of the hardest teak were built in the dockyards of Goa and Daman. One of them, the Constantina, constructed about 1550, doubled the Cape of Good Hope seventeen times and lasted twenty-five years.

I have said that the Portuguese had a coast-line of over fifteen thousand miles to hold in Asiatic waters. But their fleet enabled them to choose any point along that line for attack, and to concentrate on it their whole force. They could deliver their blow at their own time; if successful they left a garrison; if unsuccessful they disappeared below the horizon, having struck terror, or sometimes compelled submission, by the atrocities inflicted for resistance. The whole coast of Asia from the Red Sea to the Eastern Archipelago was thus menaced by an invisible foe from the ocean, whose movements defied calculation, whose attack was often irresistible, and whose vengeance always cruel. No such fleets had ever been seen in Asia, and the Portuguese treaties took care that none should grow up. As Portugal never acquired inland territories in India proper, and as her possessions were mainly confined to patches on the seaboard, this system sufficed for their defence long after her military vigour had declined. But its effectiveness depended on the absence of any other naval force; and when the maritime nations of northern Europe broke in upon the Indian Ocean, the Portuguese power collapsed.

It would be wrong, however, to underrate either the skill or the heroism with which their sea-power was built up. Thom the orders of King Emmanuel in 1514 for an examination of the ports, anchorages, and distances in the Red Sea and Persian Gulf, marine surveying dates in Asia. In spite of discrepancies in the results, a mass of material was collected during the next century, and geographical names attest the exploring activity of Portugal from the coast of Africa to China and Japan. The knowledge thus acquired was put to good use for purposes of strategy. The Portuguese found they could command the whole Asiatic trade-route by squadrons at three points on its course – the outlet of the Red Sea, the passage round Ceylon, and the Straits of Malacca. When Aden, which would be as a "key in the hands of Your Highness," could not be captured, the fortress island of Diu became to the Portuguese, from 1535 onwards, an Aden nearer to their Indian base. Its naval station caught the Red Sea and Persian Gulf ships as they rounded the peninsula of Kathiawar toward the Indian coast. Portugal thus held the three angles, at Diu, Ceylon, and Malacca, of the great triangle whose two southern sides formed the route of the spice trade.

The naval advantages won by Portuguese strategy were maintained by Portuguese valour. Whether the native powers covered the sea with their small craft, or strengthened their fleet with a huge junk carrying one thousand fighters – "the most monstrous thing that was ever seen by man, and took three years to make" – they went down before the galleons and caravels. The bare official narratives of such encounters read like epics in epitome. A captain whose coat of mail caught in the pegs as he leapt on an enemy's ship, there remained till he was hewn to pieces through his armour. Another Portuguese vessel "they made a porcupine of" with fiery darts and "assegais" heroic self-sacrifices, and deaths worthy of Sir Philip Sidney.

But the Portuguese did not trust alone to strategy or valour to secure their supremacy along the Asiatic trade-route. They boldly struck into the wars and intrigues of the native princes from Africa to the Moluccas, securing substantial returns for their support, and finding in each dynastic claimant a steppingstone to power. In 1505 Almeida drove out the ruler of Quiloa on the African coast and set up his own nominee. In the same year the Portuguese killed the King of Sofala on that coast and controlled the succession. In 1510 Cochin on the Malabar coast became the arena of intrigues between Albuquerque on the one hand and the Zamorin of Calicut on the other; Albuquerque expelling the Zamorin's candidate and re-establishing the titular raja of Cochin. In that year also, Albuquerque successfully supported one brother against another for the chiefdom of Onor, the price being submission to the King of Portugal. In 1511 he agreed to aid the King of Pacem in Sumatra against a rebellious governor, on the king's offering to become a vassal of Portugal. Albuquerque not only entered into the family intrigues of native states, but he adopted their methods. In 1513 the Zamorin of Calicut was hostile, his brother friendly, to Portugal. Albuquerque offered, if the brother would poison the Zamorin, to secure for him the throne; and the compact was duly carried out.

An eloquent essayist has ascribed to Dupleix the original idea of building up a European power in Asia by taking advantage of the rivalries of native princes, and by the employment of disciplined native troops. Such a statement merely shows that India, while within the ample range of Macaulay's genius, lay outside the area of his exact knowledge. More than two centuries before the Frenchman reached India, the design had been deliberately formed and successfully carried out. Affonso de Albuquerque claimed no credit for the discovery; he merely extended the policy of his more commonplace predecessors, and handed it on to successors who worked out its natural development. Almost any one of their intrigues might, with a change of geographical names, stand for an intrigue of Dupleix. To cite but a single example: in 1521 the Portuguese having agreed to reinstate a Sumatra king who had been expelled, overthrew and killed his rival, and secured their own nominee on the throne in return for his submission to Portugal.

The idea of employing disciplined Indian troops and of using Indian succession contests, as engines for European aggrandizement, was not struck out by the wit of any one man. It was the necessity of the European position in Asia, and it was recognized as such by the Portuguese from the moment they secured a footing on. the Malabar coast. The Indian anarchy from 1500 to 1550, which preceded the firm establishment of the Moghul empire, gave them half a century to carry out their design. The grasp of the Moghul empire after 1550 held such schemes in abeyance during nearly two hundred years. The fall of the Moghul empire rendered possible a revival of the old Portuguese policy, and from the struggle which ensued, England emerged the sovereign power in India.

The drain upon Portugal for her armies and fleets in Asia, although far beyond her normal resources, was for a time richly repaid by the monopoly of the Indo-European trade. The volume of that trade may be inferred from the statements that 806 Portuguese ships were employed in it between 1497 and 1612, and that the ordinary cost of construction and equipment of a single vessel intended for India, with the pay of the captain and crew for one voyage, was calculated at £4076. Such returns do not include ships captured in Asiatic seas or built in Indian dockyards, and, assuming their accuracy, the total number of vessels engaged in the trade can scarcely have been less than one thousand during the century of the Portuguese monopoly. The annual fleet which brought home the Indian cargoes numbered, in the palmy days of the Portuguese commerce, twenty sail. Regarding the value of the trade it is more difficult to form an estimate. . To the Portuguese cavaliers and chroniclers the achievement of their nation in India was a romance of military prowess and of missionary zeal. The commercial aspects they kept as much as possible in the background. Indeed, Faria y Sousa apologizes for referring to the expeditions of certain years, as "what they did was in relation to trade, a subject unbecoming a grave history." We have to trust to accidental notices rather than to continuous statements.

I have mentioned that the first cargo brought home by Vasco da Gama was reckoned to have repaid the whole cost of the expedition sixty-fold. Cabral returned to Lisbon in 1501 with a freight of precious spices, perfumes, porcelain, pearls, rubies, and diamonds. In 1504 Albuquerque followed with "forty pound of pearls and four hundred of the small, a diamond of wonderful bigness," and other costly articles. The gains of trade were augmented by the profits of piracy – for every Moslem or heathen ship was a fair prize. A single Cali-cut vessel in 1501 yielded, among other treasure, 1500 costly pearls. In 1503 another capture contained "an idol of gold weighing thirty pound," with emeralds for eyes, a huge ruby on his breast, "and part of him covered with a cloak of gold set with jewels." In return for gems and for the pepper, ginger, cinnamon, mace, nutmegs, cloves, drugs, dyes, porcelains, . perfumes, carved work, art products, and textile marvels of the East, the main commodity sent from Portugal, as from the old Roman empire, was silver. But she also exported woollen fabrics, to a large extent woven from English fleeces on Flanders looms, linens, red cloth of state, Genoa velvets, cutlery, metal work, hardware, corals, glass, mirrors, and chemicals.

Besides the direct commerce with Portugal, the port-to-port trade from the Malabar coast to the Persian Gulf on the one side, and to Malacca and the Far East on the other, yielded large returns. One of its most profitable commodities was opium, obtained from Arabia and Egypt. Opium had been known in China from at least the eighth century A.D., and Duarte Barbosa found the Chinese junks taking it in the time of Albuquerque as a return freight from Malacca.

It soon appeared that opium could be grown in India, and Francisco de Albuquerque proposed in 1513 that its importation from Arabia should be prohibited or should be made a monopoly of the Portuguese sovereign, as is shown by letters still preserved among the manuscripts of the India Office. When the supply was cut off in reprisal for the Portuguese attempt on Aden, Affonso de Albuquerque recommended "the poppies of the Azores to be sown in all the fields of Portugal," "because a shipload would be used yearly in India, and the cultivators would gain much, and the people of India are lost without it if they do not have it to eat." It was not on the soil of Portugal, however, that the wealth of Asia was to be reaped. Nor did the attempts to reach the inland gold-fields of Africa, although led by a captain-general bearing the lofty title of "Conqueror of the Mines," yield permanent results. The plunder of the Moslem ships, tributes and ransoms from the coast-chiefs, and above all sea trade, formed from first to last the revenue of Portugal in the East.

As regards the home trade, one Portuguese ship brought back a freight worth, at a moderate computation, £150,000, besides jewels not reckoned in the account. As regards the port-to-port trade in Asiatic waters, the voyage from Goa to China or Japan yielded to the captain for freight alone £22,500, and from Goa to Mozambique £5400; besides the gains from his private trade, which were equally great. As regards the profits of piracy, or the seizure of non-Christian ships, a single captain sold prizes during the space of two years aggregating about £110,000. The tributes from coast-princes and the customs dues of Goa, Diu, and Malacca alone were estimated at about £120,000. The king's share in the tributes, customs, and prizes taken by his own ships was reckoned at 1,000,000 crowns a year, say £225,000, and would have been double that amount, but for the frauds of the officials. His actual clear revenue from India was given at £154,913.

The trade profits to the royal treasury should have been enormous, but were reduced by the many hands through which they passed. The Portuguese sovereigns were willing to allow their subjects to benefit by Eastern commerce. Prince Henry the Navigator had, in the first half of the fifteenth century, encouraged a company formed for trading with his discoveries on the African coast. It soon became evident that the fifteenth-century world could not be opened up by private enterprise. The African and Canaries trade became a monopoly of the royal family, and merchants engaging in it had to take out a license and render a part of their profits to the sovereign or his representative. A charter of June 29, 1500, shows that on the finding of the Cape route Ring Emmanuel in like manner offered to share the Indian trade with his subjects, on condition that one-fourth of the returns should be paid to his Majesty. Again, however, private enterprise proved unequal to the task, and for the next eighty-seven years the trade of India was conducted at the risk and for the behoof of the sovereign. The royal monopoly of spices alone was estimated at £45,000 a year, and his Majesty's profit from the general trade at £150,000. Adding this to the £225,000 from prizes, customs, etc., the king's share should have amounted to £420,000 a year. But the profits were eaten up by the expense of the armaments.

The king, however, still desired to interest his subjects in the enterprise. In the second voyage of Vasco da Gama (1502), each mariner and officer of the Indian fleets was allowed to bring home for himself a certain quantity of spices, paying as freight one-twentieth of their value. A similar policy of permitting their crews "to load some small thing in their cabins," and a modest percentage on the profits of the voyage, was afterwards advocated for the port-to-port trade in Asiatic waters. Such a system could perhaps be kept under check in the return fleets to Lisbon. At the distant Indian harbours it defied control, and quickly grew into a competing private trade on a great scale. The sweets of sudden and surreptitious wealth turned the Portuguese officials into unscrupulous adventurers, careless of their master's interest in their own haste to be rich.

The abuses incident to such a system fill many pages of the letters home, as a search through the records of the India Office proves. As early as 1513 a cavalier was charged with fraudulent dealing in the rice required for the Portuguese Government. Of two galleons allowed for the king's trade, one was lost through overloading, while the captain freighted the other with his private cargo. Certain of the ships sent "to guard the mouth of the Strait" will, the king was informed, "after selling their rice depart full of gold, and will not care a straw for our service." A practice arose of coercing the coast rajas into vending their spices to the officials engaged in private trade, while the king's ships could obtain freights only at enhanced rates. Pressure was put on the native merchants, and several ports were almost deserted by them, as they had to pay heavy dues, which the Portuguese captains corruptly evaded. "The whole [royal] trade is being lost which afforded the revenues of your factory. Your Highness has not nor will have from Malacca any profit as long as the trade is being done by the captains" – who would not pay the customs levied from the Gentiles and the Moors. Such is the statement in a letter for the king from Affonso 'Alexia, dated January 15, 1530. Many other letters tell the same story. It was felt to be irregular, however, to employ as ambassador an officer who had bought up all the merchandise in the town,

and who seems to be going rather to do his own trading." Native vessels, on arriving at a port, were not allowed to sell their cargoes until the factory had bought what it wanted to make up the king's shipment, and this royal privilege the Portuguese officials converted into a device for buying on their own terms the commodities for their private trade. The result was thus pithily summed up in a communication from Fernando Nunes, September 7, 1527: "The native merchants neither will give to, nor have any trade with, your factory, from which proceeds great loss to your Highness."

These were acknowledged abuses. But apart from such abuses, the system led to a perpetual conflict of interest between the royal trade and the officials as private traders. The commanders in charge of the king's ships sold their private cargo first, and secured a return freight for themselves, before disturbing the market by transactions on his Majesty's account. In 1530 the Bengal voyage from Malabar yielded the captain £2450 and only £78 to the king – a flagrant case reported to Lisbon. The royal trade to Ormuz on the west and to Malacca on the east suffered from the same cause, as "the captains buy and sell their own goods and not for the king." The "gift of a voyage" became a recognized quittance for pay withheld or embezzled by the treasury officers, and with good luck in prizes might mean a fortune. It also formed a provision for a clamorous kinsman or a cast-off mistress, and one governor was reported to have appointed forty of his relatives to charges and voyages.

This system, from the first disastrous to the royal trade, soon proved also a source of political weakness. As early as 1524 complaints arose that the captains "do not want war, as it is too expensive and bad to endure, and of small gain and little advantage." In 1542 a new governor found the royal service in great straits, owing to the number of officers who had left it to turn merchants – a business which "offered greater chance of profit and less danger to life and limb."

After three years' experience he was anxious to resign, "as he saw around him only corruption and dishonesty." In 1549 a confidential report thus summed up the position: "Each one considers only himself."

The Portuguese sovereigns did not see the wealth of Asia thus slip through their fingers without efforts to check the malpractices in the East. At one period, indeed, they attempted to exclude not only their own servants but also the native merchants from any share in the trade. This close system, when strictly enforced, drove the Asiatic ships from the Portuguese harbours. For a time it threatened ruin to the lucrative horse trade of Goa, which imported the fine breed of the desert in Arab vessels and resold the animals at a great profit to dealers from the inland courts of India. During the cold season of 1521–1522, the usual supply of about a thousand horses had dropped to under a hundred in the Goa market. "How can your Highness expect the merchants of Ormuz to bring us horses," says a plain-speaking correspondent, "if they cannot trade in supplies or in any other commodity?" "Your Highness, by wanting to take all to yourself, nevertheless derives no advantage."

While so strict a monopoly kept away the native merchants, it merely shifted the private trade of the Portuguese officials to harbours which were less closely watched. "Your factory at Cochin," adds the same writer, "is always in debt;" the captains of the said vessels that come here making themselves very rich." The native merchants "will lose what pleasure they had in trading." "Let your Highness order your ships to be laden and command the ports to be opened" to native vessels. "There are none now, because your Highness wills to close the ports" – except to your own trade.

An attempt to remedy this state of things by granting passes to native ships, and by forbidding trade to officials, proved unavailing. The pass-system opened up a wider scope for private trading, by allowing the Portuguese servants of the crown to employ native craft to carry their own ventures. By a proclamation of 1524, the penalty to a native captain found in Indian waters without a Portuguese license was death and seizure of his ship and property. The officials took care, before granting the permit, to secure a lion's share in the profits of the voyage. Every one, sometimes the governor himself, was in the conspiracy, and prosecutions merely strengthened it by the judicial sanction of acquittals. "Which thing did not astonish me," wrote a candid observer, Limao Botelho, in 1548, "because the procurator of your Highness is one to get his salary."

The Portuguese sovereigns were, in fact, unable to check the corruption even of the Indian Department at Lisbon, and proved powerless to control their distant servants in the East. After the union of Portugal with the Spanish crown in 1580, the drain of the Netherlands war crippled the public funds required for the Indian commerce, and in 1587 the royal monopoly of the spice trade was sold to a body of capitalists under the name of the Companhia Portugueza das Indias Orientaes. The officials in Asia, fearing the loss of their illicit gains, threw every obstacle in the way, and the speculation did not yield the hoped-for profits. In 1697 a new syndicate, called the Companhia do Coramercio da India, received a charter in return for a yearly subvention of £2763 to the crown. After a four years' struggle with the officials in the East this undertaking also collapsed. The attempts of Portugal to found an East Indian Company failed, but they gave a hint to Europe as to the possibility of corporate private enterprise in Asia – a hint of which the Dutch and English availed themselves.

The Portuguese officials in India defended their clandestine commerce on the ground of the insufficiency of their salaries. Da Gama's and Albuquerque's companions had gone forth as crusaders and cavaliers, with little thoughts as to the wages of their service. Their aim was glory or death in a holy war. But the love of fighting spent itself, and the "martyrs" soon wanted pay for their "blood." At first they looked chiefly to prizes at sea, to the plunder of captured towns on shore, and to the gifts of native princes, voluntary or enforced, at every port from the African coast to the Moluccas. These gifts, originally intended for the king, were diverted to his servants, and soon grew into bribes. In 1522 his Majesty was urged to substitute fair salaries for such gratifications, which already interfered with the course of justice. But the Lisbon government could never make up its mind to this course. The European "soldiers were miserably paid and miserably fed, the captains receiving each a salary of twelve shillings per month, and living only on rice and fish." A commander of a ship of war, rejoicing in the lofty title of Capita.° de Mar e Guerra, was paid "less than a Dutch sergeant." The sea-captains did not suffer, however, as they exercised some control over the local treasuries. They paid their own claims, whether there was much or little left in the coffer, and seized the best part of the goods of patients who died in the hospitals. In 1530 the Malacca coast was left without a sufficient guard, "because in it there are no fifths and perquisites, nor what to claw, as there is in other voyages."

Some of the Portuguese exploits form a very romance of robbery. One free-lance, Nicote, having taken service under the sovereign of Pegu, rebelled against his master, was proclaimed king, and was finally impaled in front of his own fort in order, as the Burmese sarcastically remarked, "that he might the better look to it." The island which Sancho Panza hoped for, and received, as a reward for his services, has been cited as an invention out of keeping with the realism of "Don Quixote." But more than one incident in the Asia Portugueza of the sixteenth century may have supplied the idea for Sancho's Barataria. In the middle of that century Jordao de Freitas, having "converted" the King of Amboyna, obtained the island as a gift to himself. Islands were cheap in the boyhood of Cervantes. Indeed, John Cabot, when exploring the Atlantic for England in 1497, had set the example by giving away an island to his Genoese barber – who ever afterwards regarded himself as a count.

If the system produced bitter fruits in Asia, it had its roots in Portugal itself. Not only could the Lis-bon court never screw up its courage to give fair commercial salaries for fair commercial work, but it used India as a refuge for depraved or destitute hangers-on upon its bounty.

As the slave-tillage of Portugal concentrated large tracts among a small body of great proprietors, the lesser nobility and gentry sank into-indigence. Their blood disdained the degradation of trade at home, and the antechambers of the grandees were besieged by poor relations clamouring for employ-ment or bread. India seemed to offer, if not a fortune, at any rate a grave. In either case the suitor was got rid of. It became the asylum for those who had claims that could not be satisfied, or who had rendered services that could not be acknowledged, or had received promises that could not be fulfilled. Young women were shipped off from Lisbon with the dowry of an appointment in India for the man who would marry them. One favoured damsel carried in her trunk the governorship of Cranganore. The multiplication of offices was pushed to an extent which would have been ludicrous, if it had not proved fatal, in Portuguese India. But even nominal posts could not be invented to keep pace with the demand. Each of the four outward ships of a single year "brought sixty persons, more or less, without pay."

The ravenous hordes thus let loose on India made the race-name of Christian (Firingi2) a word of terror – until the strong rule of the Moghul empire turned it into one of contempt. Their buccaneering in the narrow seas, their pirate nests on the Bay of Bengal, their plunder of the coast and island princes, lie beyond the scope of this sketch, which merely attempts to indicate the policy, without narrating the transactions, of the Portuguese in the East. Wherever they went they snatched at riches; and even in remote China, in the presence of a power which might have crushed them like nutshells, they could not abstain from pillage. In 1527 Diogo Calvo reported that "no land is so rich as China," or could more cheaply supply the royal arsenals in India. The ports were open, but his brother is kept as a hostage at Canton on account of the Portuguese "slaying and robbing." The Indian settlements, which were the first destination of the adventurers from Portugal, perhaps suffered most. In 1549 things were going "from bad to worse" at Cochin – to use the phrase of a letter from Cosme Annes to the crown – and in 1552 the civic authorities of Goa at length laid their miseries before the king. "In India there is no justice, either in your viceroy, or in those who are to mete it out." The one object is "the gathering together of money by every means." "There is no Moor who will trust a Portuguese." "Senhor, we beg for mercy, mercy, mercy. Help us, Senhor, help us,. Senhor, for we are sinking."

Chapter 5 – England's Attempts to Reach India in the Sixteenth Century

1499–1599

The Portuguese soon found that they had other rivals in the East besides the Turks. No Christian nation at the end of the fifteenth century seriously disputed the Papal award. But England, France, Venice, and Spain scrutinized its terms with keen eyes, and tried for a share of the Asiatic trade by every means within the strict letter of the Bull and the treaties based upon it. England's century of failures, from 1497 onward, to reach India without infringing that settlement, disciplined our nation to distant maritime enterprise and forms the main subject of this chapter.

The Venetians strove to bolster up the old land routes through Syria and Egypt, as against the Cape passage, and outraged Christendom by abetting the Mamluk Sultan in his struggle with Portugal for the Indian seas. They thus retained the trade with Alexandria and the Levant – a monopoly svhich they had in time to share with the Turkey Company of England and the Mediterranean merchants of Marseilles. The Venetians realized, indeed, that the ultimate victory must be with the Cape route, and decided to divide its profits with Portugal in the West while encouraging the Turkish onset against Portugal in the East. In 1521 the court of Lisbon refused an offer of the Republic of Venice to buy up all the spices yearly brought to Portugal, over and above what Portugal itself required.

To the east of Suez, Venice made herself felt not by her actual presence, but by her intrigues. In the Indo-Portuguese archives she appears vaguely as an ill-wisher to Portugal and a confederate of the Turk. The Indian letters to Lisbon report such incidents as the arrest of a seditious Venetian pilot, or the apostasy of a Venetian who had turned Moor; rumours of joint preparations by the Turks and Venetians against the Portuguese; and apprehensions of the Turks and Venetians lest Portugal should block their Red Sea route by the capture of Aden. Of the French we hear little in the Indo-Portuguese records during the sixteenth century except that "the French will be ill-advised if they come seeking us."

Spain proved a more serious rival. The demarcation Bull of 1493 overlooked the fact that the earth is a sphere. The Portuguese had, indeed, only to pursue their discoveries far enough to the east of the dividing line, and the Spaniards to push theirs far enough to the west, in order that the two nations should meet angrily on the other side of the globe. This they did in 1521. Magellan, disgusted by the ingratitude of Portugal for his services under Albuquerque in the East Indies, offered in 1517 to find out for Spain a new road to Asia. Starting from Seville with five ships in 1519, he coasted down the American continent till he discovered the straits which bear his name. Then striking northwest across the Pacific he made the Philippine Islands, where he was killed in 1521.

But his squadron proceeded to the Moluccas, which had already been reached by the Portuguese via the Cape of Good Hope. One ship of Magellan's five succeeded in returning to Seville in 1522, having sailed round the world and thus opened a lawful route for Spain into the East India seas.

When the consternation of the Lisbon court calmed down, the difficulty was found susceptible of diplomatic settlement. The Bull of 1493, in partitioning the undiscovered world between Spain and Portugal, started from an imaginary line in the Atlantic. It implied, however, a complementary line half-way round the earth, say 180 degrees distant, as the boundary of the two nations in Asiatic waters. But the sea mathematics of that age were unequal to the accurate determination of either line, although the second Borgian map in 1529 attempts to show both. Charles V of Spain had, as emperor, too many wars on hand in Europe to wish for further complications in the East. He possessed, moreover, in America, an India nearer home: an India which, instead of draining the mother-country of specie every year to carry on trade, was beginning to pour into her treasury inexhaustible stores of silver. Charles V wanted the sinews of war, and he could not pay his armies in nutmegs and cloves.

Notwithstanding his promise to the Spanish Cortes in 1523, during the first enthusiasm of Magellan's discoveries, to defend them, Charles V in 1529 sold his claims to the Moluccas for 350,000 golden ducats (say £170,000) to Portugal. By the same Convention of Saragossa he accepted an Asiatic boundary-line between the two Catholic nations at 297½ leagues east of the Moluccas, reserving to Spain the right of annulling the bargain on repayment of the money. This disposed for the time of the difficulty, and the union of the Spanish and Portuguese crowns in 1580 – solemnly confirmed in 1581 – seemed to render the settlement final.

But diplomacy in Europe proved powerless, then and for two centuries afterwards, to quell the stormy passions of European rivals in Asia. The Portuguese jealousy had already been excited by the influx into India of Castilian Jews driven forth from Spain. Albuquerque proposed to make short work with these unhappy emigrants, and asked leave to "exterminate them one by one as I come across them." On the Spaniards attempting to trade at the Moluccas, the Portuguese captains waited for no orders from home, and after a fierce struggle of some years drove them out. In 1528 they forced the King of Tidore, the chief sovereign in the Moluccas, to promise never again to allow the Castilians to enter his river.

The Saragossa Convention of 1529 between Spain and Portugal provided that any Europeans except Portuguese who came within the line then agreed on should be punished as corsairs. But fighting still went on between the armed merchant ships of the two nations on the Indian seas. "In this manner do we go on day by day with these dogs, enemies of our Holy Faith," a despairing Spaniard wrote of the Portuguese in 1532, "the knife forever at our throats, swallowing a thousand deaths."

The struggle flickered out only after the native princes surrendered their islands to the Portuguese or bound themselves by treaties absolutely to exclude the Castilians from their ports. At length in 1545 the Christian commanders came to an agreement, each side solemnly purging itself as "blameless of the cockle which the Enemy of Mankind had commenced to sow." But the cockle of discord soon sprang up afresh. By a later treaty in the same year, the Spaniards surrendered their artillery and gave hostages as a guarantee that they would really evacuate Tidore; while their soldiers were offered service under the Portuguese. The monopoly of the two Catholic nations in the East, thus established, was destined to be drawn still closer by the union of the Spanish and Portuguese crowns in 1580.

The attitude of England to Portugal seems, on the other hand, to have been cordial. Ten years before the finding of the Cape route, the old friendship between the two nations had been cemented afresh, in 1489, by a "ratification of the Perpetual Peace." When, therefore, our Henry VII, inspired by Da Gama's discovery, determined to explore on his own account, he was careful to respect the rights of his "dearest brother and kinsman, the King of Portugal." In 1500 and 1502, in granting somewhat wide charters to certain Bristol and Portuguese adventurers to sail under the English flag into all heathen countries of the seas, and to erect his royal banner on whatever island or continent they should discover, Henry VII expressly provided that they should not intermeddle with the possessions of the King of Portugal or any other friendly Christian prince. Spain and Portugal, secure in the Papal award, looked on unperturbed, and in 1521 Henry VIa entered into a compact with the two nations against their common enemies and those of Christendom. In 1527 Charles V, Emperor and King of Spain, is said to have offered to sell his claims to the Moluccas to Henry VIII. This possible cause of a quarrel with Portugal came to nothing, and in 1529 the dispute between the two Iberian kingdoms was adjusted, as we have seen, by the Convention of Saragossa, while Henry VIII joined with them in negotiations for a general peace of Europe and league against the Turk.

The truth is that England believed herself on the eve of discovering a nearer way to India than either the Straits of Magellan or the Cape of Good Hope. In 1476 a Danish (or Polish?) pilot, John Scolus, is reported somewhat obscurely to have got to the passage north of Labrador, and, as Sir Clements Markham writes, "in 1477 Columbus himself learned from English sailors of Bristol the management of an ocean voyage, when he visited Ultima Thule" (Iceland). In 1480, a vessel of eighty tons sailed from Bristol under Captain Thylde, the pioneer of continuous English exploration, to discover a land to the west of Ireland called "Brasylle" – the Irish O'Brasil or Island of the Blest. He failed, but according to the Spanish ambassador, the Bristol merchants sent out two to four vessels every year from 1491 to 1498 on the same search.

When, therefore, Columbus believed he had found a way to India south-west across the Atlantic in 1492, and mistook Cuba for Japan, the Bristol merchants redoubled their efforts by a north-western route across the same ocean. All such expeditions assumed the rotundity of the earth, and the vagueness of the Papal Bull of 1493, which embittered the relations of Spain and Portugal, gave cover to the English proceedings. That Bull excluded intrusion only toward "the west and south," explicitly repeating these terms four times over, and making no reference to discoveries by the north.

The practical monopoly of Spain was to reach India by a southwest route; the practical monopoly of Portugal was to reach India by a southeast route; the English resolved to find India by a north-western or north-eastern passage. Spain saw that this might lead to an infringement on the Portuguese claims and on her own, but she did not press the point so as either to threaten a rupture or to prevent the English voyages.

Indeed the Bull of 1493, by referring exclusively to discoveries toward the west and south, left the north open; and the Spanish ambassador himself ad-mitted that the Bristol merchants had been yearly exploring in that direction before the Bull was granted. "You write that a person like Columbus," runs a letter to him from their Catholic Majesties in 1496, "has come to England for the purpose of persuading the king to enter into an undertaking similar to that of the Indies, without prejudice to Spain and Portugal. He is quite at liberty." The ambassador had been sent to England to negotiate a marriage between Princess Katherine of Spain and Arthur, Prince of Wales. In the previous decade Henry VII missed the offer of the Genoese Columbus, which would have made England the discoverer of the south-western route. In 1496 he granted letters patent to the Genoese Cabots – John and his three sons – to sail under the royal flag by the north, east, and west. The south is significantly omitted from the license.

John Cabot, a Genoese by birth but a naturalized citizen of Venice, appears to have visited Mecca, had sojourned in Portugal and Spain, and settled in Eng-land. With the aid of the Bristol merchants and the sanction of King Henry's patent, he at length set forth from the Severn on May 2, 1497, in one small vessel, the Mathew, with a crew of eighteen, of whom seventeen were Bristol men. He hoped to reach Asia by the north Atlantic, as Columbus was then supposed to have reached it by the south, and "to make London a greater place for spices than Alexandria." He returned on August 6th, having in reality discovered North America, but in the opinion of his contemporaries having gained for England "a great part of Asia, without a stroke of the sword."

Slowly and with much reluctance did England abandon this belief. Yet the voyages of 1498, 1500, 1502, and subsequent years made it evident that America was not Cathay. The latter name, Cathay or Cataya, the old land travellers had vaguely applied to Tartary and China. In the sea voyages now to be described, it included also the northern shores of Asia. A copious and contentious literature has grown up on the pretensions of Sebastian, son of John Cabot, to have been the true discoverer of North America, and on his, perhaps juster, claim to have definitely given shape to the conception of a northwest passage to India. The idea of such a passage took possession of the stubborn English mind.

Of the resolute efforts to convert that idea into an accomplished fact I can narrate only the most memorable, drawing from the Calendar of State Papers and from Hakluyt's Voyages. In 1527, Master Robert Thorne addressed a book to Henry VIII's ambassador at the court of Charles V, urging the King of England to become a merchant like the King of Portugal, and advocating in great detail the north-western route. His father was one of the discoverers of Newfoundland, he himself had dwelt in Seville and adventured 1400 ducats in the Indo-Spanish fleet of 1527, with which sailed "two Englishmen sent to discover 'the Islands of the Spiceries.'"

"Now then, if from the said New Found Lands the sea be navigable," he argued, "there is no doubt but sailing northward and passing the pole, descending to the equinoctial line, we shall hit these islands, and it should be a much more shorter way than either the Spaniards or the Portugals have." He estimated the length of the Spanish route by the southwest Atlantic at 4200 or 4300 leagues, while the English route by the northwest would be only 2480 leagues. Two ships were despatched in this year, including, according to Hakluyt's account, the Dominus Vobiscum – "The Lord be with you." One of the vessels perished off Newfoundland; the other returned, leaving the possibility of a north-western passage much as it was before.

A more persistent attempt was made in 1536 by Master Hore of London – "a man of goodly stature and of great courage and given to the study of cosmography." With him went "many gentlemen of the Inns of Court and of the Chancery, and divers others of good worship desirous to see the strange things of the world" – sixty men in all, of whom thirty were well born. Starting in April, 1536, from Gravesend in two small vessels (one of 120 tons) they reached the coast of Newfoundland. There the crews were driven by starvation to eat each other's flesh. In vain Hore upbraided them "in a notable oration, recounting how these dealings offended the Almighty." They cast lots as to who should next die, but "such was the mercie of God that the same night there arrived a French ship in that port well furnished with victual, and such was the policie of the English that they became masters of the same, and changing ships and victualing them, they set sail to come into England." The haggard survivors reached Cornwall in October, 1536, so worn by hunger and misery that one of them could not be recognized by his own father and mother save by a wart on his knee. The French captain, whom they had plundered, afterwards appealed to Henry VIII. His Majesty, however, was so moved by the sufferings of the English crews "that he punished not his subjects, but of his own purse made full and royal recompense unto the French."

The next expedition which must be noticed was the famous one of Sir Hugh Willoughby in 1553 to find a passage by the northeast. Sebastian Cabot stands arraigned as a disloyal son who filched his father's achievements to fabricate a reputation for himself. But he was also a skilled geographer and an indefatigable projector of voyages. Born in Bristol, and associated with his father in the patent of Henry VII for the expedition which in 1497 discovered North

America, he became dissatisfied with the meagre rewards of Henry VIII for his map-making, and about 1513 repaired to Spain. There he found employment under King Ferdinand as a cartographer and member of the Council of the New Indies.

After various vicissitudes, during which he retransferred his services to England and back again to Spain, Sebastian Cabot finally returned to England in 1547, and gained distinction as arbitrator in an old-standing dispute between the London merchants and the Hanseatic colony of Germans in that city. When further consulted by the London merchants as to the depression of trade, due to the disturbed state of Europe, he advised them boldly to strike out a path for them-selves northeast to Asia, and under his impulse, on December 18, 1551, what is in reality the first English East India Company was formed. Its capital consisted of £6000 in £25 shares, with Sebastian Cabot as governor for life, and eventually twelve councillors for the voyage.

The daring project met with impediments, and it was not until May, 1553, that the little squadron could start. It consisted of three ships of 160, 120, and 90 tons, each with a pinnace and boat. Its object was "the discovery of Cathay, and divers other regions, dominions, islands, and places unknown." It carried a complete set of instructions "by the Right Worshipful Master Sebastian Cabota Esquier, Governor of the Mystery and Company of the Merchants. Adventurers of the City of London," and letters from "the Right Noble Prince Edward the Sixth, sent to the kings, princes, and other potentates inhabiting the northeast parts of the world." We shall see that this double precedent of mercantile ordinances and royal missives was followed by the more permanent East India Company of 1600. Sir Hugh Willoughby, Knight, commanded as admiral or "Captain General," and Richard Chancelor went as pilot-in-chief.

Into the controversy which surrounds this voyage I need not enter. It suffices for Willoughby's fame that he was the first Englishman to reach Nova Zembla; that the results of the expedition led to an overland trade by way of Russia into Asia; and that he laid down his life in the attempt. From August 23 to September 18, 1553, Willoughby coasted the shore of northern Russia with two vessels of the squadron, and tried to explore inland. Here his diary comes to an abrupt close, although it would appear from a will that he was alive as late as January, 1554. In that long winter darkness he and the crews of his two ice-bound ships – about seventy men in all – perished of cold and starvation, freezing to mummies as they died. The next explorer found the weird company about two years later, Willoughby still sitting in his cabin with his diary and papers before him. A strange fate befell the poor corpses on the attempt to bring the vessels home, for we are told by the great Puritan writer John Milton, in his History of Muscovia, that "the ships being unstaunch, as is supposed by the two years wintering in Lapland, sunk by the way with their dead and them also that brought them."

Richard Chancelor, the second in command, had got separated from Willoughby in a storm off the Lafoden Islands. He eventually reached Archangel, and obtained from the Russian sovereign, Ivan the Terrible, a grant of freedom of trade for English ships. On his return a new company was formed to take advantage of this grant, with a charter from Queen Mary in 1554, under the title of "the Merchant Adventurers for the Discovery of Lands, Countries, Isles, etc., not before known or frequented by any English." Persons not members of the company nor licensed by it, who should venture into the Russian dominions, were to forfeit their ships and merchandise, one-half to the English crown and one-half to the company. The monopoly grew into the powerful organization known as the Russian or Muscovy Company, which by many voyages, perils, and diplomatic arrangements, established a trade through Russia to Persia; was a rival of the great East India Company; and lasted till toward the end of the eighteenth century.

This sea-and-overland expedition by the northeast had been chartered by Queen Mary in 1554 for the purposes of trade as well as of discovery. I must not pause to relate how Chancelor and Burrough promptly started in 1555–1556 to open up the path, or how its agent Anthony Jenkinson reached Moscow in 1557, dined with the Tsar "at six o'clock by candle-light," and penetrated to Bokhara, where he met the traders from India and Cathay. It was not an overland route, but a northern passage by sea that had taken hold of the English imagination; and the trade by way of the Volga and the Caspian formed no answer to the problem which English seamanship had set itself to solve.

The death of Queen Mary put an end to constraints that had arisen out of her Spanish marriage, and with the accession of the Protestant princess in 1558 a host of projectors appeared. A rivalry sprang up between the advocates of the northwest and the northeast passage. In 1565 Anthony Jenkinson urged on Queen Elizabeth a northeast exploration by sea "to set forward this famous discovery of that renowned Cathay." In 1566–1567 [Sir] Humphrey Gilbert wrote his noted Discourse "to prove a passage by the northwest to Cathay and the East Indies," and offered to find it by the "travel hazard and peril of my life," on condition that he and his heirs should be secured in the fruits of the discovery.

But the great north-western attempt of Elizabeth's reign was the three voyages of Frobisher. Martin Frobisher, merchant, mariner, and on occasion corsair, had for fifteen years nourished a scheme for a passage northwest to Cathay. On his travels he met with Michael Lok, an adventurer equally daring, a more exact student of geographical science, and possessed of wealth earned by sea-trade. Lok's father, while on business at Dunkirk in 1533, had torn down the Papal Bull excommunicating Henry VIII, rose into high favour with that sovereign, became alderman and sheriff of London, and died as Sir William Lok in 1550. His son Michael having commanded a ship of one thousand tons in the Levant, and, being stirred by "the great traffic into the East Indies" which he had seen in Spain, financed Frobisher's first voyage.

After unsuccessful negotiations with the Muscovy Company, a charter was obtained from Elizabeth in February, 1575, for a northwest expedition in favour of Lok, Frobisher, and such others as would adventure. Lok subscribed £738 of the total £1613 required, and on June 12, 1576, their two little barks of twenty-five tons each, with a pinnace of ten tons, and thirty-four persons all told, sailed from Gravesend under Frobisher's command. The pinnace was soon lost, one of the barks parted company in a storm and came home, but Frobisher went on, entered the straits to which he gave his name, and returned to Harwich on October 2, 1576 – bringing great hope "of the passage to Cataya which he doubted nothing to find and pass through." Among his trophies were an Esquimaux with his canoe, whom he had enticed to the side of his little vessel, then stooping over the side had with his own arms "caught the man fast and plucked him with main force, boat and all, into his barque."

Frobisher also brought home certain pieces of stone which an Italian assayer, Agnello, declared to contain gold. Money was quickly forthcoming for a second voyage at a cost of £4500; the queen subscribing £500, afterwards raised to £1000; the lord treasurer, lord admiral, and other high officers £100 each. Even Philip Sidney caught the fever and put down for this and the next voyages £25, then £50: modest sums, but apparently beyond the young poet-courtier's purse, as he figures in 1579 among the adventurers who had not paid their subscriptions – a defaulter for £77.

Frobisher's second expedition, consisting of his former two little barks with "one talle shippe of her Majestie," started on May 26, 1577. His hope was to pass into the "Mare Pacificum or Mare de Sur by which he may go into Cataya, China, the East India, and all the dominions of the great Cane [Khan] of Tartaria." But his fixed resolve was to find more of the gold-bearing stone. On September 23 he returned to Milford Haven, bringing home a quantity of the supposed ore, went to court, and received from Queen Elizabeth great thanks and most gracious countenance." The new northern land discovered on this voyage her Majesty named the Meta Incognita – the Unknown Turning-post into Asia – and designed to send thither chosen soldiers and discreet persons to form a settlement.

The hope of gold now wrought like a frenzy. It seemed as if England had within her grasp not only a passage to the East Indies about half as short as the Spanish route, but also stores of bullion which would reduce to contempt the silver of Spanish America. A German assayer, Schutz, engaged that two tons "shall yield in fine gold" twenty ounces, and although the mint officials gave no certain sound, it was resolved to secure at once five thousand tons of the ore. "The northwest passage is almost wholly lost sight of," says Mr. Sainsbury in summarizing the State Papers; "gold is the pith, heart, and core of most of the correspondence."

On May 31, 1578, Frobisher sailed on his third voyage from Harwich with eleven ships. The queen herself graciously wished him farewell at Greenwich. He carried the hopes and fears alike of the city and the court; and the divine blessing was sought by strict articles "to banish dice and card playing" "and to serve God twice a day, with the ordinary service usual in churches of England." The password for the crews was "Before the world was God;" the countersign, "After God came Christ his Sonne." Amid tempests and ice dangers so dire that Frobisher, "when all hope should be past ... resolved with powder to burn and bury himself and all, together with her Majestie's ships, and with this peal of ordnance to receive an honourable knell" – the fleet secured its cargo of ore, and returned to England on October 1, 1578.

The gold mania rushed to a climax. Wild rumours spread as to the value of the freight; an ominous silence followed, then angry fears. Finally in 1583 the assay of William Williams proved that two hundred weight of "Frobisher's ore" yielded but two minute particles of silver, not the size of a pin's head, which were fastened with sealing-wax to the margin of the report. The three voyages had cost £20,160; involved terrible sufferings in stormy and ice-bound seas, and left ruin behind. Frobisher seems to have adventured what little he had, and in 1577 (?) his wife represented her hard fate to Secretary Walsingham as "your humble oratrix, the most miserable poor woman in the world." A widow of good estate when she married Frobisher, she and her children were in a wretched room at Hampstead ready to starve, and she prayed for help in collecting an old debt of £4 to save them from famishing.

The miseries of Michael Lok were more drawn out. He had contributed or truly expended £6250 on the three voyages – he declared to the Privy Council in 1579 –"all the goods he hath in the world, whereby himself, his wife, and fifteen children are left to beg their bread, except God turn the stones at Dartford into his bread again." No miracle took place. After lying long in the Fleet Prison and failing in attempts to re-establish himself in life, Lok was in 1614–1615, at the age of eighty-three, still being prosecuted for debts incurred for the Cathay Company thirty-five years before.

Meanwhile English exploration had not stood still. As the great struggle with Spain drew on, the Protestant spirit of England rose, and in 1578 Drake broke into the Pacific by the south-western route and visited the Moluccas, all Papal Bulls notwithstanding. Elizabeth hesitated to follow up to its mercantile uses her privateering hero's voyage round the globe (1577 1580). But during the recriminations which ensued with Spain, she found it necessary to challenge the Catholic monopoly of the Asiatic trade based on the Papal settlement of 1493. The Pope's award became a disputed "donation of the Bishop of Rome." "The use of the sea and air," she argued, "is common to all," "as neither nature, nor public use and custom permitteth any possession thereof." Drake's voyage into the forbidden oceans, and Elizabeth's challenge of the international system on which the interdict rested, opened up possibilities of a southern passage which the East India Company, twenty years later, turned into facts.

These possibilities and the ruin and discredit in which Frobisher's search for gold had ended, somewhat abated the national interest in the northern routes. But expeditions still went on. In May, 1580, the Muscovy Company sent out two vessels of forty and twenty tons, the joint crews numbering but fourteen men and two boys, to discover a north-eastern passage to the "dominions of the mighty prince, the Emperor of Cathay." One of the little barks, under Jackman, perished at sea; the other, under Pet, discovered the straits which bear his name between Waigatz and Russia, but was forced back by ice and returned to England in December, 1580.

After much negotiation a fourth voyage was entrusted to Frobisher, which marks the growing resolve of England to penetrate to Asiatic seas by the forbidden southern route. Its object was to "be only for trade and not for discovery of the passage by the north-east to Cataya," unless the information could be incidentally obtained. Frobisher declined the command, and in June, 1582, the ships sailed under Captain Edward Fenton with designedly ambiguous instructions. "You shall take your right course to the isles of the Moluccas for the better discovery of the northwest passage," provided that the discovery may be made "without hindrance of your trade;" and also to find a north-east passage if, on the same conditions, he could. The main idea seems to have been to reach the Moluccas by the Cape of Good Hope, or if needful by the Straits of Magellan, to open trade and to establish small settlements at places, to fight the Spaniards if attacked, and to inquire whether the northern passages which had defied all efforts from Europe could not be opened out from Asia. It was a vast enterprise, with a squadron of four ships aggregating 740 tons, besides pinnaces and shallops, provisioned for thirteen months, and with a subscribed capital of £11,600, of which £2000 were invested in merchandise.

After a year's absence Captain Fenton returned to Plymouth in May, 1583, with a sad tale of failure. He has been accused of deviating from his instructions. with the design of seizing the Island of St. Helena, "theire to be proclaimed Kyng." It is certain that he took six months to reach Brazil. Contrary winds and want of victuals, he wrote to Burleigh, then prevented him from passing the Cape of Good Hope, while the news of a great Spanish fleet at the Straits of Magellan deterred him from attempting that route. He decided to traffic, or buccaneer, along the coast of Brazil; fought a battle with a Spanish squadron; and came back with the empty words that, but for these mishaps, he dared well assure the lord treasurer they had brought home in honest trade above £40,000 or £50,000.

As a matter of fact, he bartered away one of his ships to the Portuguese, lost another at the River Plate, quarrelled with his officers, buried forty-five of his men, and did nothing. It still took men of the Drake and Cavendish stamp to break into the Indian seas. But the union of the crowns of Spain and Portugal under Philip II in 1580 gave a new incentive to the task. Apparently in the very year of Fenton's return, 1583, the danger to Europe of allowing Spain to enjoy both Portugal and the East Indies was publicly discussed. The remedies proposed were for England to seize and fortify the Straits of Magellan; to take and keep Port St. Vincent in Brazil, and to discover the northeast passage with all speed.

The time for these heroic measures had not come. Yet the next few years saw memorable attempts both to the north and the south. In 1585, 1586, and 1587 John Davis made his three great voyages, in each of which he felt convinced that he had found the northwest route. As the result of the first, he announced to Walsingham, on October 3, 1585, "that the northwest passage is a matter nothing doubtful, but at any time almost to be passed, the sea navigable, void of ice, the air tolerable and the waters very deep." On returning from the third he declared, in September, 1587, "the passage is most probable, the execution easy, as at my coming you shall fully know."

Davis discovered' much, but he had not found the outlet,, and he became a mark for the scoffer. The crisis of the Spanish Armada in the following year, 1588, absorbed the whole energies of the nation, and his alleged north-western route ended in disbelief and contempt. Yet although mistaken, he was honest, and in 1595 he still held that "it seemed most manifest that the passage was free and without impediment towards the north, but by reason of the Spanish fleet and unfortunate time of Mr. Secretary's death, the voyage was omitted and never sithins attempted."

Events had taken place which fixed the eyes of the nation on a very different route. On the assumption of the crown of Portugal by Philip II of Spain in 1580, one of the rival claimants, Don Antonio, Prior of Crato, appealed to arms, was defeated, and sought shelter in England. The union of the two Iberian monarchies, with the command of the joint resources of the East and West Indies which it gave to Philip, seemed a menace to all Europe. France and England drew closer together, and Elizabeth encouraged the fugitive Antonio to the furthest limits short of a rupture with Spain. Some relief she could openly afford to an unfortunate prince in whose veins the blood royal of Eng-land, even if tainted by illegitimacy, flowed. In November, 1581, the 'Spanish ambassador gave a check to her hesitating designs and official disclaimers by demanding the arrest of the pretender. The armed ships bought for Don Antonio in the Thames, he declared, had sailed past the queen's own window at Greenwich with the flag of Portugal displayed. "Your Majesty will not hear words, so we must come to cannon, and see if you will hear them." Elizabeth, without raising her voice, told him that if he used such threats she would throw him into a dungeon. But she was not yet prepared for an open breach with Philip.

She was willing, however, to see her subjects do what she feared to undertake. The Spanish monopoly of the Magellan route had been challenged during the diplomatic wrangle arising out of Drake's voyage round the world in 1577–1580. In July, 1586, Thomas Cavendish set forth on the same course with three small ships of 140, 60, and 40 tons respectively, with crews aggregating 123 men. Philip II had attempted to forestall such irruptions into the Pacific by a fortified settlement commanding the Straits of Magellan.

But Cavendish found the miserable colonists dead or fleeing from the place, which he contemptuously named the Town of Famine. Pillaging, prize-taking, and burning to the water's edge, he raided up the Pacific coast of Spanish America, buccaneered through the Spanish and Portuguese islands of the Indian Ocean, and finally returned to England by the Cape of Good Hope with one surviving ship, in September, 1588, to be sung in ballads and flattered by the court.

Two months before his arrival Spain had struck her long suspended blow. In the summer of 1588 the Invincible Armada came and perished. Even Elizabeth felt that the time for pretences was past. In the following year, 1589, as recorded in the State Papers, she received a memorial setting forth the benefits to the realm of a direct trade with India and praying for a royal license for three ships. Leave granted, the capital was raised, and in April, 1591, the first English squadron sailed round the Cape of Good Hope into the Indian seas. One of the three ships, the Merchant Royal, had to be sent back to England from Table Bay, laden with victims of the scurvy. Of the two which sailed on, the Penelope went down in a tempest with the commodore or "General" George Raymond and all hands. But Captain James Lancaster in the Edward Bonaventure passed up the African coast to Zanzibar, crossed over to Cape Comorin, reached the Malay Peninsula, and returned by Ceylon and the Cape of Good Hope.

Atlantic hurricanes buffeted him about from the West Indies to Newfoundland and back again. While on shore with most of the crew, his sole surviving ship was blown far out to sea with only five men and a boy on board, but she at length reached England. Captain Lancaster, after generous succour from French vessels, himself arrived at Rye in 1594. Of 198 men who had rounded the Cape of Good Hope with him in 1591, barely twenty-five again saw their native land. But they brought back a precious cargo of pepper and rich booty. The only dangerous enemies they had met were the scurvy and the storm. Lancaster's voyage tore the Papal award of 1493 into shreds, and with it the charter of the Catholic monopoly in the Indian seas.

We must be careful, however, not to overestimate the binding force of the Bull of 1493. I have said that at the end of the fifteenth century no Christian nation seriously disputed the Papal award. But the outbreak of free thought during the first quarter of the sixteenth, which grew into the Reformation in Germany and England, was also represented in France by the struggle of Francis I with the Pope. The witty king among his courtiers would have liked to see the testament of Father Adam which authorized his Holiness to divide out the world. For a moment, indeed, Francis I seemed disposed to give practical effect to his jibe. The Florentine Captain Verazzani, whom he commissioned to make discoveries to the northwest, adventured about 1524 southwards within the demarcation line.

The expedition failed. The explorer was eaten by cannibals, or, as is supposed with less likelihood, was captured by the Spaniards and hanged at Madrid, and the Eldest Son of the Church never repeated the attempt. When the Huguenots became a power in France, during the middle of the century, the forward party settled colonies on the coasts of Brazil and Florida, between 1555 and 1564. But the Brazilian settlement lapsed to the Portuguese, the Florida colonies were destroyed by the Spaniards and were chiefly remembered in France as episodes in the Protestant movement. Such infringements of the Papal award formed maritime incidents of greater religious or political struggles. The punishment provided by the Bull of 1493 was excommunication; and to sovereigns like our Henry VIII, who had broken or were about to break with the Roman See on other grounds, the sentence ceased to have terrors. To James I, and to Protestant rulers like Cromwell or the champions of Flemish and Dutch liberty, the Bull was null and void.

Meanwhile the Papal settlement had passed into the public law of Europe. It is not needful here to inquire whether the Bull of 1493 was only ad spiritualia. The treaty of Tordesillas in 1494 and the Convention of Saragossa in 1529, practically, although not expressly based upon it, were diplomatic facts backed by powerful armies. If Henry VIII had challenged the principle of the Bull embodied in these instruments, he would have run the gauntlet of Portugal, Spain, and the empire. If Elizabeth had as queen openly encroached within the Spanish line, she would have had to reckon with Philip II. It did not suit her to do so until urged on by his war preparations and emboldened by the destruction of his Armada. During nearly a century England tried to reach India by every possible route not precluded by the treaties which gave effect to the Bull – through the ice-bound seas of the northwest and the northeast, overland across Russia by means of the Muscovy Company, and due east, as we shall presently find, by way of the Sultan's dominions and the Levant.

The other Protestant sea-power of northern Europe had adopted a similar policy. As early as 1565 the Dutch established a factory, or trading-post, at Kola on the north Russian route, and soon began to explore eastwards toward Cathay. Uncertain attempts, Dutch or Swedish, followed. In 1593 commenced the series of determined efforts of Holland to reach Asia by the northeast passage, which have placed William Barents in the foremost rank of Arctic explorers.

His first voyage occupied the summer of 1594, and brought him through storms and ice-floes to the Islands of Orange. On the second voyage in 1595 he found the strait south of Waigatz Isle blocked with ice, was imprisoned by the frozen masses at Idol Cape, but eventually reached Staten Island off Tierra del Fuego. Despite this achievement, the States-General decided not to expend public money on further attempts to discover a north-eastern passage, with so little prospect of a pecuniary return. But to encourage private adventurers they offered a large reward in case of success. A third expedition accordingly started in May, 1596, with Barents as pilot-in-chief, and keeping more to the north reached Spitzbergen. They were forced "in great cold, poverty, misery, and grief to stay all that winter" at the Haven of Nova Zembla, and the much-enduring Barents died on the return voyage to Holland in the following spring. By this time the Dutch, like the English, were resolved to reach India by the south, in defiance of Spanish treaties and Papal Bulls. From freedom in religion sprang the freedom of the sea.

Not only had the diplomatic settlement of the undiscovered world, based on the Papal partition, broken down, but the methods of exploration had profoundly changed. Medieval sea-trade rigorously enforced the maxims of secret commerce. Venice, like Carthage of old, punished with death the revealer of a maritime route, and the export of charts of discovery was a capital crime. The Adriatic merchants raised a wall of mystery between the Mediterranean and the Atlantic.

They "laboured to make us strangers to the Great Turk, the Egyptians, and bordering countries, and brought them to that ignorance of our nation, that they thought England to be a town in the kingdom of London," wrote Sir William Monson. In 1424 the Doge had considered a copy of the travels of Marco Polo, together with a map (probably the precious Medicean portulan of 1351) as a State gift worthy to accompany the thanks of the Republic to Prince Pedro of Portugal for his good offices in negotiating a treaty with the emperor.

This doctrine du secret commercial, which weighed heavily on early exploration, ceased to be tenable in the sixteenth century. Prince Henry's cartographical school at Sagres, in the fifteenth, had done much to render available the then existing stock of knowledge regarding the undiscovered world. But it was the application of the Flemish printer's and graver's art to map-making at the beginning of the sixteenth century that gave the death-blow to secret commerce. A magnificent school of cartography grew up at Antwerp and Bruges – a school ennobled by master-minds like Mercator, Ortelius, and De Jode, and fertile in processes of map-reproduction destined to make the discoveries of one nation the common property of all.

The Netherlands school of geographers rendered possible the developments in maritime commerce which culminated at the end of the sixteenth century in the English and Dutch East India Companies. It started from the theoretical cosmography of the Ptolemaic system, and the Roman itineraries of which the Peutingerian Tables (circ. 226 A.D.) form a striking example. To these it added the actual discoveries, and some of the conjectural errors, embodied in the mappemondes and portulans of the middle ages. The voyages of Columbus and Da Gama made the medieval charts obsolete. On the ruins of the old cosmography the Italian and Dutch map-designers built up a new geography, and the Antwerp map-printers published it to the world.

The system of secret commerce had thus to give place to a doctrine of exclusive right founded on priority of discovery. This doctrine, crudely expressed in the demarcation Bull of 1493 and elaborated by later diplomacy, gave a monopoly to the first comer. The drift of affairs in the next two centuries disclosed, however, that such national monopolies afforded no final settlement for the newly found regions of the globe. The right of discovery had to submit to modifications based on the plea of non-effective occupation. But from first to last, monopoly was the guiding principle – the monopoly secured by secret trading, the monopoly of the Papal Bulls and treaties founded thereon, the monopoly given by the right of discovery, and the monopoly derived from that right modified by effective occupation. To this long tradition of monopoly the English and Dutch East India Companies became the residuary legatees, and it profoundly influenced their whole history.

If, during nearly a century, the Portuguese maintained the monopoly of the Indian trade, they for a time enforced it in no grudging spirit toward other Christian nations. Beyond Lisbon to the south, indeed, all intruders were treated as pirates, and misleading reports were spread, according to the maxims of secret commerce, about the dangers of the route. But in 1500, immediately after Da Gama's discovery, the Portuguese king admitted naturalized foreigners to trade with the East at Lisbon itself, and he cordially entered on a project for an Indian mart in northern Europe. Bruges, the outlet to the North for the Eastern trade by thy medieval land paths, had decayed, owing partly to the blocking of the Asiatic routes by the Turks, partly to the vengeance of Maximilian of Austria for its revolts, but permanently in consequence of the silting up of its river and ports.

The Portuguese king made Antwerp the entrepôt of Indian produce for northern Europe, and the opening up of a new branch of the Scheldt, by. the scouring of the channel about 1504, gave it a sea approach such as Bruges had not enjoyed even in the height of her prosperity.

Lisbon thus became the port of trans-shipment between the East and the great colonial mart of Antwerp. During the first half of the sixteenth century England's direct traffic with Lisbon was small, although we find Henry VII granting a charter in 1500 to a joint company of English and Portuguese adventurers, and Portuguese merchants figure among the residents in London with whom the Venetians were in 1507 licensed to trade. But between Antwerp and London an enormous traffic grew up. Antwerp not only supplied England with the precious stones, fine fabrics, spices, drugs, and dyes of the East, but she took in return and distributed to Europe the raw materials and manufactures of England, as a long list of these exports and imports in 1560 shows.

In 1550 the Emperor Charles V found that the English merchants employed twenty thousand persons in Antwerp, and he refrained from imposing the Inquisition on the city, lest, it should drive the Englanders away. They did business with a Portuguese colony on the Scheldt, and no fewer than three hundred wealthy Spanish families had their domicile in Antwerp. Over five hundred vessels are reported to have sailed in or out in one day, and the ships and small craft were said to aggregate ninety-two thousand a year.

This centre of the world's traffic, Dives Antwerpia, almost at our doors, gave an impulse to the mercantile spirit in England. "Clear-sighted persons at court" advised, as early as the reign of Henry VIII, a policy of colonial enterprise in place of interference in the continental wars. "Let us," they said, "in God's name, leave off our attempts against the terra firma, as the natural situation of islands seems not to suit with conquests of that kind. Or, when we would enlarge ourselves, let it be that way we can, and to Which it seems the eternal providence has destined us, which is by sea. The Indies are discovered, and vast treasure is brought from thence every day. Let us, therefore, bend our endeavours thitherwards; and if the Spaniards and Portuguese suffer us not to join with them, there will yet be region enough for all to enjoy." For these statements we have no less an authority than Lord Herbert in the sixteenth century.

From the outset, therefore, the Indies formed the goal of English maritime enterprise in the sixteenth century. The efforts to reach that goal by a northwest or a northeast passage I have already described. But Elizabeth did not confine her attempts to the north alone. As far back as 1553 English ships began to make their way to the coast of Guinea – an infringement of Portuguese rights profitable to the Portuguese themselves, and placed on a treaty basis in 1572. The occasional seizures and reprisals which followed did not seriously disturb the amity of the two nations; and England's friendship on the Newfoundland bank was worth some concessions in the South. For the English had the best ships engaged in the Atlantic fisheries, and, although in 1577 they numbered but fifteen as against fifty Portuguese and a hundred Spanish, they were said to give the law to the rest.

Elizabeth's diplomacy enabled her adventurers to push not only southwards by Guinea, but also eastwards through the Mediterranean. In 1577, according to Sir William Monson's Naval Tracts, she sent a mission to the Emperor of Morocco, with the result that the English merchants secured a firm footing and gradually ousted the Portuguese from the trade. In 1579 her envoy to the Ottoman Sultan obtained permission for English merchants to resort freely to the Levant, and in 1581 she granted a charter of incorporation to the Turkey Company. After the joint Armada of Spain and Portugal against England perished in 1588, Elizabeth extended the scope of this corporation in 1593 to India, under the title of the Governor and Company of the Merchants of the Levant.

The union of the Spanish and Portuguese crowns in 1580 was to the Protestant sea-powers of the sixteenth century what the closing of the Eastern land routes by the Turks had been to Christendom in the fifteenth. Again a great necessity arose for a new departure in Indo-European commerce. Portugal was dragged at the heels of Spain into her suicidal grapple with the Reformation; and the Catholic monopoly of the Indian trade Went down with the Armada in the English Channel and North Sea. From the moment that Philip II added Portugal to the Spanish monarchy, the English and Flemish adventurers foresaw the end. In 1580 divers London traders petitioned the Council for Elizabeth's consent to an expedition direct to India; a year later the Dutch made a similar application to William I The life-and-death struggle which followed, by united Spain and Portugal on the one hand against England and the Netherlands on the other, was fought out, not by royal fleets and armies alone, but also by the merchants of the rival nations. The Dutch and Spanish war of commercial edicts scarcely makes itself heard in history amid the din of battle, the shrieks of street massacres, the groans from Inquisition chambers, and the inrush of the ocean through the dikes But it gave a staggering blow to the Catholic monopoly of the Indian trade. In 1585, for example, Philip II ordered the seizure of all Dutch ships in Spanish waters. The States-General retorted by forbidding any Dutch vessels to trade with Spain or Portugal under pain of forfeiting both ship and goods. If these menaces had some ring of empty shouting in front of the battle, they soon acquired a very real meaning. Spain ruined Antwerp. The States-General issued ten proclamations between 1585 and 1600 against trade with Portugal or Spain. In 1595 the States-General forbade all navigation of Dutch vessels within Spanish waters, and in 1596 sent a ship of war as far as Calais to arrest any Dutch craft on its way to Spain, Portugal, or Italy.

England, thus deprived of her Indian trade through Antwerp, had meanwhile met the difficulty in the Elizabethan fashion. The open enmity authorized by the rupture of diplomatic relations with Spain in 1584 1585, broke out into blows between a Portuguese ship of the East Indian fleet and two English vessels in 1586. In 1587 Drake captured off the Azores the San Filippe, a great carrack bearing the king's saint-name and laden with an Indian cargo which yielded

£108,049 of prize-money. In 1592 Sir John Burrough swooped down on the homeward-bound Indian ships near the Isle of Flores, drove one ashore, and took the other – the Madre de Deos, almost the largest vessel belonging to the Portuguese crown, with a cargo valued at £150,000. Such windfalls, however, proved a poor substitute for England's regular Indian trade through Flanders, now stamped to death under the heels of Spanish armies. Leave was at length obtained from Elizabeth to strike into the direct Indian trade, and in 1591, as we have seen, the first English squadron sailed round the Cape of Good Hope.

When showing how the Turkish seizure of the ancient land paths constrained Christendom to seek an ocean route to India, I added a caution not to exaggerate the effects of that single cause. So now that Philip II's crusade against the Reformation stands disclosed as a compelling influence which led the Protestant Powers of the North to break into the Eastern seas, we should not forget that it was only the last and most imperious of many influences that had been at work. At the end of the fifteenth century Portugal held a unique position, with the geographical science of the Mediterranean at her back, and the unexplored Atlantic in front. At the end of the sixteenth, owing to improvements in navigation and the labours of the Flemish map-makers, she had to share these advantages with the maritime nations of northern Europe. Sooner or later the Catholic monopoly must have collapsed. That it collapsed at the particular moment and in the exact way that it did, resulted from the same spirit of military and religious aggression to which it owed its birth. For the Portuguese Order of Christ and the conversion of the infidel, we have but to substitute the Spanish infantry of Alva and the persecution of the Protestants. The exalted fervour with which Da Gama, after his solemn vigil, received the sacred standard on the Tagus beach in 1497, breathes in Don John's ejaculation as he marched forth from Namur with the Pope's banner floating over him in 1578. "Under this emblem I vanquished the Turk; under the same will I conquer the heretics."

Not only had the Catholic trade through Lisbon and Antwerp been crushed, but the still older channel through Egypt and Venice was now closed. From the blocking of the Syrian trade-routes by the Turks in the fifteenth century to far on in the sixteenth, Venice had been a chief intermediary between England and the East. Her "argosy" to Southampton in 1587 perished miserably, and what between the anti-Catholic movement in England and other causes, the trade came to an end. It was a great ship of 1100 tons, richly laden, with an English pilot on board. The entrance by the Isle of Wight was extremely dangerous for the unmanageable monster in a high October sea, and the pilot refused to attempt it. But the Venetians compelled him by force. "When the poor man," wrote an eye-witness, "neither with persuasions nor tears could prevail, he did his best to enter the Channel of the Needles; but such was the greatness of the waves, and the unwieldiness of the ship, not answering her helm, that she struck upon the Shingles, where she, her goods, and company, except seven poor creatures, perished." So in the very autumn before the Spanish Armada strewed the coast of Ireland with her timbers, the last shipment from Catholic Venice was wrecked off the Isle of Wight.

If the destruction of the Armada threw open the ocean to the Protestant Powers of the North, Spain still remained mistress of the Mediterranean. She commanded the Straits of Gibraltar, and as the sovereign power of Sicily, Sardinia, Naples, and the Duchy of Milan, she controlled the commerce of the great inland sea. Her naval supremacy only ended where that of the Turks began. As the conflict between England and Spain became more bitter, Philip II consoled himself in some measure for the loss of the Atlantic by tightening his grasp on the Mediterranean highway. The English Levant Company, expanded in 1593 into an overland Indian company, found itself menaced. The union of the Spanish and Portuguese crowns, in this respect also, compelled the Eastern trade to seek a new route.

Among concurrent causes which led to the founding of the Dutch and English East India Companies the travels of Linschoten and Fitch held a distinctive place. From 1583 to 1589, John Huyghen van Linschoten of

Haarlem dwelt at Goa in the train of the Portuguese archbishop. A keen observer, and a Dutchman at heart, Linschoten on his return to Europe in 1592 placed at the service of his country the stores of knowledge which he had accumulated in Indo-Portuguese employ. The States-General granted him a license to publish his work in 1594, and although the First Part, or the Itinerario proper, was not completed till 1596, the Second Part, setting forth the routes to India, was available in 1595. Its effect was instantaneous. In 1595 a squadron of four ships was despatched under Cornelius Houtman "to the countries lying on the other side of the Cape of Good Hope," and the journals of the voyage show that Linschoten's sailing directory was used on board. Houtman returned in 1597, having lost two-thirds of his crews and done little in actual trade, but bringing back a treaty with the King of Bantam which opened up the Indian Archipelago to Holland.

Linschoten's work was in some sort a revelation. All northern Europe learned that the path lay open to India, and that the Indian system of Portugal was rotten to the core. English and German translations appeared in 1598, two Latin translations in 1599, and a French translation in 1610. The preface to the English edition in 1598, by W. P. (generally supposed to be William Philip), sounded like a trumpet-call to the nation, and gave a direct impulse to the founding of the East India Company. It speaks of the "great provinces, puissant cities, and unmeasurable islands" of the Indies. "I doo not doubt, but yet I doo most heartily pray," it adds, "and wish that this poore Translation may worke in our English nation a further desire and increase of honour over all Countreys of the Worlde" by means of "our Wodden Walles."

England had, meanwhile, received a similar impulse of her own, and from a native source. In 1591 Ralph Fitch returned to London with a marvellous tale of travel. The first Englishman who dwelt in India was Thomas Stephens, of New College, Oxford, 1579, unless we accept the legend of Sighelmus of Sherbourne's pilgrimage to the tomb of St. Thomas near Madras, in the reign of King Alfred. As rector of the Jesuits' College at Goa, Stephens's letters to his father are said to have quickened the desire of the English merchants for direct trade with the East. In 1583 Ralph Fitch set forth with three principal companions bearing letters from Queen Elizabeth to the King of Cambay and to the Emperor of China. They journeyed by the Euphrates valley to Ormuz, where they were arrested by the Portuguese, and carried thence as prisoners to Goa.

Emerging from this captivity in 1584, Fitch visited the court of the Emperor Akbar, in northern India; one of his companions married a native woman, another entered the Moghul service, a third had turned monk at Goa. But Fitch went on. After many adventures in Burma, Malacca, the "Golden Chersonesus," and Bengal, he again explored the Portuguese misrule in Cochin and Goa, and thrilled London in 1591 with the magnificent possibilities of Eastern commerce. The effect was, as we have seen, the expansion of the Turkey Company into an East India Company in 1593, with a charter to trade through the Grand Seignior's "countries overland to the East Indies." Its ultimate consequences were more important. Fitch had done for England perhaps less than Linschoten did for Holland. But the less sufficed.

It now became a race between England and Holland for the capture of the Indian trade. Houtman's expedition of 1595–1597, under the impulse of Linschoten, was quickly succeeded by others. In 1598 five other Dutch squadrons sailed, including the one under the famous Van Neck, whose return with more treaties and a rich freight intoxicated the nation. Houtman himself went forth on a second expedition, in which he and many others were treacherously slain. The survivors returned in 1600.

Between 1595 and 1601 no fewer than fifteen Dutch expeditions started for India by the Cape of Good Hope or the Straits of Magellan. By that time associations for Eastern trade had been formed through-out the United Provinces, and in 1602 they were amalgamated by the States-General into the Dutch East India Company.

England pressed hard after Holland, although with less certain steps. It seemed, indeed, that Captain Lancaster's heroic voyage of 1591–1594 had given the lead to our nation, and if followed up it would certainly have placed us first in the race. But Elizabeth still cherished some flickering fancies about Spain; the States-General indulged in no illusions regarding Philip II and had got beyond hopes or fears. Moreover England had rival interests – the Muscovy Company with its old route through Russia, and the Turkey Company with its new charter for trade to India by the Levant; for Holland the question was the Cape route or none. During Lancaster's absence in the Asiatic seas Elizabeth heard from Seville that, rather than let the English trade with the Indies, the Spaniards "will sell their wives and children."

However, in 1596 she consented to an expedition of three ships, mainly at the charge of Sir Robert Dudley, and gave it a letter to the Emperor of China. The little squadron under Captain Benjamin Wood was obscurely heard of in 1598 as having captured two Portuguese treasure-ships on their way from Goa to China, but not a single man returned to England to give an account of its fate. The English crews were killed off by sickness till only four men remained, and they were cast ashore on a small island near Puerto Rico. Of this miserable remnant, three were murdered by Spaniards for the sake of the treasure they had with them. The fourth, after relating his sad story to the Spanish officers of justice, was poisoned. The loss of this expedition hung like a cloud over the English merchants, while the Dutch were drinking deep to the Indian treaties and rich cargoes of Van Neck.

"Thus perished," wrote a despondent British chronicler, our "attempt to open a passage into India."

The check was only for a moment. In 1598 the English translation of Linschoten's Itinerario made the London merchants realize afresh the splendour of the prize and the certainty that it was about to pass from the Catholic South to the Protestant North. The report that the Dutch had bought up ships in England for a new voyage stung English national pride. In 1599 the London merchants gave counter-check by an enthusiastic subscription of £30,133 for an East Indian voyage, and begged the queen's royal assent to the expedition "for the honour of our native country, and for the advancement of trade of merchandise within this realm of England." The commercial rivalry between Holland and England – that rivalry which was to outlast generations, to affect profoundly the European policy and national antipathies of England, to burn British ships in the Medway, and to stamp the tragedy of Amboyna in letters of blood upon England's Asiatic history – now stood revealed.

Chapter 6 – The Constitution of the First English East India Company

1600

The English East India Company was essentially the child of the Elizabethan age. When the London merchants met together in Founders' Hall on September 22, 1599, with the lord mayor presiding, they had before them three models of Indian trade: the Portuguese royal system, the semi-State pattern of the Dutch, and the English mixed method of armed private commerce, represented in its war aspects by Drake's buccaneering adventures and in its more peaceful developments by the Levant Company.

The Portuguese system had been created by a dynasty; it was worked by, and for the benefit of, the crown. Its ships were the king's ships, its cargoes were bought and stowed by the king's people, the purser or financial superintendent of the voyage was nominated by the king's secretary, and the officers were appointed by the Admiralty. Even when the king granted a license to private merchants, as in the case of the Fuggers of Augsburg, their factors had cabins and a diet assigned to them on the royal ships. As we have seen, however, Portugal's national achievement in the East was not traffic alone, but, in the patriotic vaunt of her historian, "cities, islands, and kingdoms first groaning under our feet, and then worshipping our Government." Such a system of direct dynastic trade was alike alien to the genius of the English nation and to the caution of Queen Elizabeth.

The Dutch model came nearer to English ideas. During the long struggle with combined Spain and Portugal, the Dutch had to pay their armies and to feed themselves by sea-trade. How Holland, whose wind-swept fens did not yield crops to keep the people alive for much more than half the year, accomplished this feat, and turned her despairing land revolt into a triumphant oceanic war, forms a brilliant chapter in European history. Her national safety so vitally depended on maritime trade, that it became as clear a duty of the Dutch Government to promote private commerce as it was for private commerce to fight the battles of the republic. The States-General not only subsidized expeditions of discovery, but when the failure of such expeditions compelled them to withhold direct support from the public purse, they still offered a large reward to private adventure.

This semi-national character stamped itself almost, although not quite, from the first on the Dutch East India Company. The Dutch voyages "to the countries lying on the other side of the Cape of Good Hope," which we have seen inaugurated by Houtman in 1595, were at once recognized as attacks upon united Portugal and Spain. In September, 1598, great preparations against the Flemings in the Indian Archipelago were reported from Lisbon to Cecil. This was no mere "Portugal brag," as the correspondent supposed. During the previous summer Philip II had ordered his Indian fleet to close in on the Hollanders at the Straits of Malacca, and to impress whatever private shipping might there be found to aid in their destruction. Portuguese influence with the native princes was to be vigorously directed to shut out the Dutch. No wonder the separate states of Holland felt that something more than their individual support to the various Dutch companies was demanded. In 1602 all the local groups of the East India adventurers in the United Provinces were amalgamated into one powerful company by the States-General with the enormous joint capital of 6,500,000 florins, say £540,000, if we take the florin at twenty pence at that time, and administered under the supervision of a central board of representatives from the subscribing states.

This nationalizing of the Dutch East Indian trade carries us three years beyond the meeting of the London merchants in September, 1599. But from Houtman's first voyage in 1595, the influences which rendered such a centralization inevitable were at work in Holland. Before describing the feebler corporate system which the English adventurers worked out for themselves, it is needful to understand what a united East India Company on the Dutch quasi-national basis really meant.

The States-General, in reorganizing the East India companies of the several States into one association in 1602, granted to the new body corporate the exclusive right of navigation to the east of the Cape of Good Hope and to the west of the Straits of Magellan for twenty-one years. The chief shareholders were the great merchants of Amsterdam and of the other subscribing States, but all inhabitants of the Low Countries were, on payment, entitled to join. The republic vested in the company the power to make war or peace, to seize foreign ships, to establish colonies, construct forts, and to coin money. On the other hand, the States-General enforced from the company not only an oath of fidelity and certain customs-dues, but also the right to call for and supervise its accounts. The whole charter reads like a Protestant counterpart of the privileges granted to Portugal by the Bull of 1493, except that religious proselytism drops out of view, a commercial company takes the place of the king, and instead of the poena excommunicationis latae against rivals or intruders, we have the direct arbitrament of the sword.

This strongly knit corporation had a governing body not unworthy of its national character. The board consisted of sixty directors, assigned to the several states in proportion to the subscriptions received from them. It was closely connected, both in the person of its directors and in its public policy, with the States-General. Hardly had it been established than it began to build forts in the East, to appoint governors, and to make treaties with native princes in the name of the stadt-holder of Holland.

I have passed on three years beyond the English proposals of 1599, in order to give a connected view of the constitution of the great rival company with which the London adventurers were des-tined from the date of their first actual voyage (1601–1603) to contend.

The London merchants who met together under the lord mayor in Founders' Hall in September, 1599, had no such ambitious scheme of an official organization in their minds. They sought a remedy for a block that had taken place in the Indian trade. Their Muscovy Company, dating from Queen Mary's charter in 1554, had failed to establish a direct overland commerce with India, and even its dealings with Russia and north-eastern Europe had of late dwindled away. Sir Walter Raleigh lamented that formerly "we sent store of goodly ships to trade in those parts, and three years past we set out but four, and this last year two or three." The Dutch have gained all the foreign freight, "whilst our ships lie still and decay, or go to Newcastle for coals."

The other English route to Asia, represented by the Turkey or Levant Company, had during the same period met with great difficulties. What the pirates of the Caspian and the Tartars of the Volga were to our Muscovy Company, the Barbary corsairs and the fleets of Philip II proved to the Levant corporation. The Barbary corsairs were bought off by large sums, amounting in one year to £2000. The gauntlet of the Spanish navy had also to be run, and in 1590 our homeward Levant squadron of ten vessels forced their way through the Straits of Gibraltar only after a pitched battle with twelve great Spanish ships. His Catholic Majesty could grip our Mediterranean trade by the throat in the passage between Spain and Africa, as he hoped to strangle the Dutch trade in the narrow seas of Malacca. So highly did the Dutch rate the difficulties of our Mediterranean route that in 1597–1599 they raised the price of pepper against us from 3s. to 6s. and 8s. per pound, and other spices in proportion.

Influential members of the Levant Company, thus finding that their extended charter of 1593 availed little for an overland trade to India, led the movement in September, 1599, for a voyage direct round the Cape. That movement, although it derived a patriotic impulse from the Dutch purchase of ships in London for their Indian expeditions, seemed to spring out of the embarrassments of our Mediterranean trade. Among its most active promoters were Richard Staper and Thomas Smythe, two of the original founders of the Levant Company. Richard Staper is described in the first charter to the Levant Company in 1581 as having, with Sir Edward Osborn, "at their own great cost and charges found out and opened a trade to Turkey," "whereby many good offices may be done for the peace of Christendom, relief of Christian slaves, and good vent for the commodities of the realm." At the beginning of 1599, Richard Staper and his associates in the Levant Company "engaged Mr. Mildenhall, a merchant of London, to go to the court of the Great Mogul," with a view to open up the Indian trade. In September of the same year Staper appears in the first list of subscribers to the East India voyage, in the first list of committees or directors, and as constant in his attendance at their meetings or "courts."

Thomas Smythe, also named as a founder of the Levant Company in its charter of 1581, was appointed the first governor of the East India Company by its charter of 1600. Many other directors or servants of the East ,India Company were, or had been, engaged in the affairs of the Levant Company. Indeed it ap-pears that the new company at first entered its proceedings in one of the record books of the old, and "that the book originally belonged to the Levant Company, but was afterwards used by both companies in common." If this statement goes a little too far, the evidence tends to show that "the East India Company was partially an outgrowth of the Levant Company."

It was an outgrowth that at first seemed destined to be nipped in the bud. The more ambitious of the 101 merchants and citizens who put down their names for £30,133 on September 22, 1599, contemplated a single voyage to begin with, but not a single voyage alone. Three days later they resolved to ask the queen to grant them "a privilege in succession and to incorporate them in a company, for that the trade of the Indias being so far remote from hence, cannot be traded but in a joint and a united stock." They also prayed for her assurance that their ships, when ready, should not be detained on plea of the public service; for a privilege to export foreign coin or its equivalent from the realm; and for freedom from export-customs on the goods sent forth by their first six voyages.

Queen Elizabeth, ever the lady patroness of private adventure, signified her gracious assent to certain of the promoters "who have bene at ye Court." But her Privy Council held back. In the previous year, 1598, France had made a separate peace with Spain by the Treaty of Vervins, and Elizabeth was by no means anxious to be left sole champion of the Netherlands' cause. It seemed indeed as if the Anglo-Spanish war, which had dragged through the fourteen years since 1585, was at last about to close. Accordingly, the Privy Council threw over the East India adventurers, rather than risk a new grievance to Spain. On October 16, 1599, it refused the privileges they sought, so as not "to forego the opportunity of the concluding of the peace. Whereupon the adventurers "resolved to postpone their voyage to more propitious times.

Meanwhile they set to work to make out a good case for a grant of privileges on a wider scale. This incapacity for knowing when it was beaten appears throughout the whole career of the company. If it succeeded or if it failed, it went on. The adventurers drew up an ingenious document intended to gain their point whether the peace was concluded or not. They asked the Privy Council to require from the Spanish com-missioners a list of all Spanish possessions east of the Cape of Good Hope. Foreseeing that Spain would not consent to this, they themselves set down the names of twenty-one places, from Sofala on the East African and Diu on the northwest Indian coast, to Macao in China and Manila in the Philippines, to which they admitted the Spaniards and Portuguese had a right. "Yet there remaineth," they went on to say, as recorded in the State Papers, "that all the rest rich kingdoms and islands of the East, which are in number very many, are out of their power and jurisdiction, and free for any other princes or people of the world to repair unto."

Of these they enumerated seventeen countries or kingdoms, from Madagascar off Africa to "the rich and golden island of Sumatra," "the most mighty and wealthy empire of China," "and the rich and innumerable isles of the Moluccas and the Spicerie." Their list acknowledges the Spanish claim to the old Portuguese settlements on the western coast of India, and to Tidore and Amboyna in the Moluccas. But it claims Bengal, Java, and the Eastern Archipelago in general as still open to the world. "In all these and infinite places more, abounding with great wealth and riches, the Portuguese and Spaniards have not any castle, fort, blockhouse or commandment." The memorialists cite in support of their case twelve Portuguese, Spanish, and Italian authors of European repute, besides nine English and Dutch. Their most important piece of evidence was "the notable intercepted Register, or Matricola, of the whole government of the East-India, [captured] in the Madre de Deos, 1592."

The document ignored the Papal partition of the world in 1493, together with the treaty settlements based upon it, and recognized only the title of effective occupation. It marked an earlier stage of the ideas which received their full development in Cromwell's attack on San Domingo half a century later, on the ground "that the said island was not entirely occupied by Spain." The "Bull must be trampled underfoot," Sir John Seeley remarks of this development in 1654, "Protestant Englishmen must assert their right of settling and acquiring territory." It is needless to say that Spain was not in 1600, nor for many years to come, prepared to accept this new departure in international law. What the memorialists then asked was that Spain should schedule her Indian settlements on the assumption that all the East that was not in her actual possession lay open to the world.

Queen Elizabeth, while perhaps smiling at the short cuts of merchant diplomacy, gravely referred the memorial to the learned Fulke Greville. His reply to Sir Francis Walsingham does not carry the case much further, but it forms the masterpiece of East Indian political geography in the Elizabethan age.

Taken along with the map of the world in 1600 – Shakespeare's "new map with the augmentation of the Indies," scored over by lines and curves like Malvolio's fantastically smiling face in "Twelfth Night" – it marks the exact point which English knowledge of the Asiatic seas had reached, when the East India Company started on its independent career of maritime discovery.

Such academic dissertations, however interesting to posterity, little affected the policy of the moment. In 160,0 the Spanish negotiations came to nothing, and the English adventurers ceased writing minutes and began to buy ships. They had, as a body, remained in abeyance from October, 1599, to September, 1600, yet the prompt action which followed their next general meeting shows that their leaders had not been idle. The discussions of the intervening months had opened a grander vista of Eastern enterprise alike to the nation and the crown. It was no longer a question of a voyage or voyages, but of an armed and chartered monopoly for the permanent Indian trade.

Having at length received the queen's assent, the adventurers reassembled in Founders' Hall on September 23, 1600, exactly a year after their first abortive start in 1599. They at once appointed a committee of seventeen, including Alderman Thomas Smythe and Mr. Richard

Staper of Levant Company fame, to ar-range for the voyage. Next day the committee proceeded to Deptford and bought the Susan, of 240 tons for £1600; and within a week the Ascension, of 260 and the Hector of 300 tons. A pinnace, the Guift of 130 tons, was afterwards purchased for £300 as a victualler to accompany the fleet, and to be cast off at sea at the discretion of the commander. But the adventurers wanted something more powerful than ordinary trading craft, and on October 7, 1600, after a good deal of haggling, they bought for £3700 the Mare Scurge, a warship of six hundred tons, from the Earl of Cumberland, who had built her to prey upon the Spanish trade. This strongly armed cruiser, under her changed name of the Red Dragon, finally The Dragon, became the flagship of the company. Her refitment was pushed on with vigour, the committee providing a barrel of beer daily for the shipwrights, so that "they leave not their work to run to the alehouse."

It soon appeared indeed, that, during its year of silent incubation, the enterprise had altogether outgrown its original scale. A much larger capital would be required for the voyage, and the £30,133 subscribed in September, 1599, had to be more than doubled to £68,373 before the expedition set forth. So great a sum could be raised only by the help of a royal charter wide in scope and continuous in character. The petition of 1599 to the queen for a warrant to fit but ships and to export bullion would not now suffice. It had developed into a scheme for incorporation somewhat on the model of the Levant Company, but with larger powers, a wider area of business, and a longer term of monopoly.

On December 31, 1600, Queen Elizabeth granted a charter in this sense, "for the Honour of our Nation, the Wealth of our People," "the Increase of our Navigation, and the advancement of lawful Traffick to the benefit of our Common-wealth." It constituted the petitioners into "one body corporate and politick, in deed and in name, by the name of the Governor and Company of Merchants of London trading into the East Indies," with legal succession, the power to purchase lands, to sue and be sued, and to have a common seal. It vested the management of the company in a governor and twenty-four committeemen, who were to be annually appointed in July, the first set being named in the charter, and including Thomas Smythe as governor and Richard Staper, the two original founders of the Levant Company who had most actively promoted the new East Indian enterprise.

The charter secured, for fifteen years from Christmas, 1600, the exclusive privilege of the Indian trade, that is with all countries beyond the Cape of Good Hope and the Straits of Magellan, except such territories or ports as were in the actual possession of any Christian prince in amity with the queen (unless by his consent), to the body corporate, and to their sons not being under twenty-one years, their apprentices, factors, and servants. It also empowered the Company to make by-laws, and to punish offenders against them by fine or imprisonment, as far as consistent with the laws of the realm. All the queen's subjects were prohibited from trading within the geographical limits assigned to the company, unless under its express license, on pain of forfeiting ship and cargo, imprisonment, or other punishment.

So far the charter provides for the creation and management of the company, its continued existence for fifteen years, its powers to hold property, its right to trade to any country of the Indian seas not in actual possession of a friendly Christian prince, its exclusive privilege to do so as against all other subjects of the queen, its power to grant licenses of internal trade to outsiders, and to discipline by fine or imprisonment its own members and servants for breaches of its by-laws. The charter ignores the Spanish claims, founded on the Bull of 1493, but respects rights derived from actual possession – the position taken by the adventurers in the previous year.

These powers, as against third parties, foreign or domestic, were supplemented by considerable privileges as against the crown. The queen, considering the hazards of an untried trade, and the company's ignorance as to what English goods would be vendible in India, exempted from export duties the outward cargoes of the first four voyages, and allowed six to twelve months' credit for the payment of the customs on their home-ward freights. Indian goods brought by the company might, after once paying the import duty, be re-exported without further dues. For the first voyage the company might export Spanish or other foreign silver coin and plate to the amount of £30,000, but in the case of subsequent voyages the company must reimport within six months the equivalent of the silver exported by it. As the nature of the voyage compelled the ships to start at a particular season of the year, the charter provided that, even "in any time of restraint," the company should be empowered to send forth annually "six good ships and six good pinnaces well furnished with ordnance and other munition for their defence, and five hundred mariners, English men," unless the queen required them for her own service. If the trade proved unprofitable to the realm, it might be revoked on two years' notice from the crown; if beneficial, the charter should be renewed on the expiry of the fifteen years for another like period.

The body corporate thus created represents both as to the nature of its business, and as to the mechanism for conducting it, the final stage of sea-enterprise in the Elizabethan age. As regards the nature of its business, Elizabethan maritime adventure had started with voyages mainly of discovery, but with an eye also to the Indian trade. Such voyages are summed up in Frobisher's north-western expeditions (1576–1578), beginning in exploration and ending in a gold mania. They developed into the voyages, partly of discovery though chiefly for plunder, of whose corsair-commanders Drake forms the heroic figure-head. But side by side with these buccaneering ventures grew up more peaceable yet armed enterprises whose chief, if not sole, object was trade. Of this last class the Levant or Turkey Company long survived as the type. The East India Company exemplifies that type of armed sea-trade on its largest scale, and with the fullest powers of expansion and of self-defence.

So also in regard to its working mechanism the East India Company stands to us as the final expression of the co-operative principle in the Elizabethan period. From the very first, as noted in the Court Minutes, September 25, 1599, the adventurers declared "that the trade of the Indias being so far remote from hence cannot be traded but in a joint and a united stock." From the first also they insisted that the contributions of members should be in money, and not in kind; that neither ships nor goods should be accepted from any adventurer "as his stock" or in lieu of his subscription in cash. A corporation so constituted seems closely to resemble a modern joint stock company, but the resemblance is by no means complete. Its nature was rather that of a modern syndicate formed to obtain from the crown a concession of the East India trade for a certain number of years, and then to work the concession by means of successive new syndicates or groups of subscribers from among its own members for separate voyages, but under its corporate control.

In such latter-day comparisons, however convenient for illustration, there lurks a constant source of error. For the institutions of Elizabethan England were formed not on new patterns for the future but upon the models of the past. The East India Company, like the Levant or Turkey Company, was built on the deep foundations of medieval trade. It proceeded on the principle that the protection of trade formed a duty of the sovereign, that protection involved regulation, and that it was beneficial for the nation that each trade should be placed under a guild or corporation with powers of self-management and internal control. Such guilds, while generally deriving their authority from the crown, were chiefly composed of the members Of a specific trade, and were designed to defend its interests. No citizen could practise the incorporated trade or craft without being admitted a brother of the guild. But every member once admitted was free to set up business on his own account. A medimval town was thus honeycombed with a number of little coipora-tons, each having the monopoly and management of a separate trade, but whose members were all at liberty to trade for themselves under rules formed for their common good. These early attempts to combine the strength of co-operation with freedom of individual initiative survive, after many metamorphoses, in the London City companies. Their modern representatives, in an active state, are "Lloyd's" and the Stock Exchange.

As handicrafts grew into manufactures, and as trade expanded into commerce, the system developed into corporations for foreign enterprise, such as the Merchants of the Staple, the Fraternity of St. Thomas a Becket (afterwards the Merchant Adventurers), and the Muscovy Company. Each company held a charter from the sovereign creating it a corporate body and assigning to it the exclusive privilege of a certain class of business, with powers to regulate the conduct of the business in the common interest of the members. While the stability of corporate management was thus secured, the individual liberty of each member was generally maintained, down to the time of Queen Mary. But the sea-commerce of Elizabeth, especially during the long state of war with Spain from 1585 to her death in 1603, demanded the strength of a closer union. Her last great charter, that of the East India Company, marks the final stage of the process. It gave powers as ample as ever from the crown to the corporate body, but it further fortified those powers by curtailing the individual liberty of the members. The corporate body could alone send forth voyages, and could alone conduct them, the separate members could no longer trade on their own account. The loss of private initiative was the price paid for the increased strength of corporate action.

The East India Company may thus be regarded as the mercantile expression of those forces of union which so profoundly modified our national growth under Elizabeth. Yet it was in no sense a national enterprise, or a semi-national association like the Dutch East India Company. The queen allowed a private group of her subjects to adventure their capital in the East India trade, and granted them such privileges as did not interfere with her own foreign policy. When their interests clashed with her foreign policy, she did not hesitate to withdraw her support, and the adventurers had to wait a year, after receiving her gracious assent, until the failure of the Spanish peace negotiations gave her once more a free hand.

While, however, the company was not a national one, it drew its very existence from the royal prerogative. Not only did its monopoly as against all other English subjects, its partial exemption from customs, and its right to export bullion depend on a grant from the crown, but it had to invoke the aid of the crown in the daily conduct of its business. No single voyage could be equipped without a separate commission from the sovereign. Warrants from the lord treasurer for the passage of victuals from port to port, or for re-straining the sale of pepper until the king's stock should be disposed of, and royal warrants for each separate voyage, occupy many pages of the records. Even in its internal management, the directors (or "Committees ") were constantly running to the Privy Council whenever a difficulty arose. Thus if defaulters would not pay up their subscriptions to a voyage, or if a further subscription were required, or if coercive powers were needed to float a northwest expedition, or if carpenters had to be pressed for fitting out the ships, or if an unsuccessful captain had to be dealt with, it was to the Lords of the Council or My Lord Treasurer that the company applied. It was also from their lordships, and My Lord Admiral and Mr. Secretary, that the company received rebuke for slackness in its duties.

The "Company of Merchants of London trading into the East Indies" was, therefore, in many senses a "Regulated Company:" regulated as to its general powers by royal charter; regulated as to each particular voyage and as to its internal management by the' Privy Council and the crown; very strictly regulated as to its individual members by its own governing body, consisting, under the charter, of the governor and twenty-four committee-men. It thus stands as the perfected type of the Regulated Companies which formed the intermediate link between the mediaeval trade guilds, and the modern commercial associations under the Companies' Acts. The personal independence of members of the earlier Regulated Companies was transferred from the individual member to the group of subscribers to each voyage. Their liability was limited to their individual subscriptions. Yet the company, acting as a whole, could increase the amount of a separate subscription by a pro rata levy, to meet the requirements of the voyage. For the first voyage, for example, an extra call of 2s. in the pound was made, according to the Court Minutes of April 1, 1601; and in all a levy of 4s. in the pound above the subscribed sums was made, according to the Minutes of July 6, 1601. These levies required for their enforcement the aid of the Privy Council.

This early form of limited liability and joint stock has never, so far as I am aware, been examined from the actual records of a corporation. Adam Smith's classical passage still forms the best account of the Regulated Company. But his reflections are biassed by a misconception as to the origin of such privileged bodies. "In the greater part of the commercial states of Europe," he writes regarding the protection of trade by the ruling power, "particular companies of merchants have had the address to persuade the legislature to intrust to them the performance of this part of the duty of the sovereign, together with all the powers which are necessarily connected with it." Such eighteenth-century philosophizing does not sufficiently allow for the natural development of the Regulated Company from the medieval trade guild, a development not due to the "address" of "particular companies of merchants," but a necessary adaptation of old forms to the growing requirements of trade. Instructive as are Adam Smith's historical sections on Regulated Companies, they are from an outsider's point of view.

I intend, from the contemporary records of the East India Company, to show the actual working of the Regulated system in its mature Elizabethan growth. Admission' to the "one body corporate and politic" of "the Governor and Company of Merchants of Lon-don trading to the East Indies," might be obtained by purchase of a share in a voyage, or by redemption, or by presentation, or by patrimony, or by apprenticeship. The last four methods require few words. Admission by patrimony, that is of sons of members on reaching twenty-one years of age, and by apprenticeship, was provided for in the charter. Apprenticeship also came to include foreign employment, as in the case of Samuel Husbands, "in regard he had served the company ten years in India." The apprentice or servant, on admission, paid a small sum, from ten to forty shillings, for the poor. In the case of sons born after their father had ceased to be a member, admission was "of grace, not of right," and on payment of a fine say of £10. Admission by presentation or a faculty, "for the making of a free man," was occasionally granted to some nobleman or powerful member. Admission by redemption became common when the company got into low water, and grew anxious about keeping up its numbers. Under this system it admitted members for such cash payments as it could obtain. In 1619 the rate was confirmed at £100. During the distresses of the civil wars the price fell to £5, and in October, 1647, fifteen new members were admitted for that modest sum.

The usual method of admission was by purchase of a share in a voyage. The subscribers to the first voyage were practically the petitioners for the Charter of 1600, and they were included by name in the charter as forming the company, or were afterwards incorporated into it, "in as large and ample manner," "as if their names had been contained in the patent." The amount of contribution which entitled a subscriber to the freedom of the company (or one "share") was originally £200. For the second Cape of Good Hope voyage in 1604 the minimum share was fixed at £100. But this arrangement threw undue power into the hands of small holders at meetings of the General Court of proprietors. Of the 205 subscribers to the third voyage in

1607, a majority of 108 were for sums under £200. The company resolved, therefore, to strengthen the hands of the leading members who had a serious stake in the business, and raised the minimum subscription to £500 in the fourth voyage of 1608. To induce small capitalists to come forward, however, they were allowed to join their subscriptions under the name of one person who had the right to vote for an aggregate stock of £500. The "share" or amount of capital which thus entitled a subscriber to the full privileges of a Freeman, and therefore' to a vote, varied at different periods. In 1619 it was £100.

In a certain sense, therefore, the company was identical with the subscribers to the first voyage, and it had a capital of £68,373 subscribed for the voyage. But as soon as it expended that capital on the first voyage, from which no return could be expected for several years, it ceased as a company to have any capital of its own for further voyages. Its business was, there-fore, to plan voyages, to obtain the royal sanction. for each voyage, and to recommend each voyage for subscription to its members, to receive the subscriptions as a separate fund applicable to the particular voyage, to buy ships and goods for the voyage, and finally to divide the profits among the individual group of sub-scribers who had found the capital for the separate voyage.

Putting all this in very modern terms, the company was, as I have said, a syndicate with a concession for the Indian trade during fifteen years, and it worked its concession by forming minor groups, theoretically among its own members, to find the capital for each separate voyage – the management of all the voyages remaining in the hands of the parent syndicate, and the liability of the minor groups being limited to the separate voyage to which they individually subscribed. Their liability might, however, be extended to a forced contribution to a further venture, if fresh capital could not be raised from a new group of subscribers.

To any one accustomed to work a limited liability association under the Companies' Acts this system bristles with divided interests. As a matter of fact, it in time developed a complexity which ultimately destroyed it. But to its Elizabethan founders it seemed simple enough. When the money subscribed for a particular voyage had been invested, and the ships sent out, the company usually rested awhile from its labours. Then the "Committees," or some enterprising member, started a project for another voyage, and a general court was held to consider the proposal. If agreed upon, "a title or preface" to a new "book of contribution" was drawn up setting forth the objects of the voyage and the capital required for it. Members present who wished to join the fresh venture put down their names for various sums; and the book was then delivered to the beadle "to be carried to all the several freemen of this fellowship to set down their several adventures in" the "voyage." The beadle went round with the book, and if he brought it back with a full subscription list, good and well. If not, certain influential brethren, practically the directors or committeemen, were appointed to take it round again to the members, and "to persuade and encourage them to proceed in the said adventure." In some cases the contributors to one voyage were induced or compelled to provide the capital for another. Thus, the subscribers of the first voyage had to submit to a pro rata levy for the second; and the subscribers of the third voyage had to take up the fifth and share the profits of the two.

The capital for a further voyage having been provided, the company bought the ships and goods for the voyage, drew up instructions for its conduct, and obtained the necessary powers from the crown for sending forth armed vessels, marines, and silver specie or coin from the realm.

This complicated business was mainly conducted by the governor and committee-men, whose "Court of Committees" resembled the board of a joint stock company at the present day-. As the arrangements advanced, they were laid before a general court of the company presided over by the governor and attended by the committee-men, "with the greatest [or greater] part of the generality."

Very strict by-laws regulated these meetings. The beadle could be sent to summons any brother of the company (usually a defaulting subscriber), and the meeting or "court" fined him a shilling for non-appearance, or sixpence should he come late. If he proved obstinate, a warrant for commitment from the Privy Council brought him to reason. No brother could speak above thrice' on any matter "upon pain of forfeiture of 3s. 4d. for every such excess in speech." The fine for interrupting another brother in his lawful discourse "by whispering speech or talk" was 2s. 6d., while "any uncivil or intemperate speeches or behaviour" were punished by a mulct of 10s. No brother could leave a meeting without permission before its close, under penalty of a shilling. Above all, "when Mr. Governor or his deputy commandeth silence by stroke of the hammer" let every one hold his peace "upon pain of forfeiture of sixpence." These fines, the precautions of serious citizens for the orderly conduct of their business, were enforced by sending those who would not pay them to prison, "there to remain during the pleasure of the generality."

The record for the equipment of each voyage may be reduced in most cases to four documents. In the first place, there was the Royal Commission of Queen Elizabeth authorizing the company to undertake the individual expedition, and vesting in its commanders powers for punishing offences during the voyage, and for the "quenching of all such mutiny, quarrels, or dissensions that shall or may" arise.

In the second place, the company issued a commission or code of instructions to the "General" or Admiral, and to the commanders of the ships, setting forth in great detail the scope and objects of the voyage, together with minute regulations for its conduct and trade. In the third place, Royal Letters Patent authorized, when needful, the coinage of money or export of specie for the voyage. La the fourth place, Letters Missive were sought from the sovereign to the foreign kings, princes, and potentates at whose ports the ships were to trade. A curious circular letter of introduction from Elizabeth "to the Great and Mighty King of ___" leaves the address blank, to be filled up and delivered at the discretion of the commander of the expedition. The subsequent letters from King James are usually directed to specified princes in the East.

These four instruments stand out as landmarks of the separate voyages above a mass of correspondence and detail. The example of a single voyage must serve to illustrate the routine proceedings for its sanction and equipment. Three months after the first voyage round the Cape of Good Hope, set forth (as we shall see) from Torbay on the 22d of April, 1601, the company received a letter from "one George Waymouth, a navigator," proposing a voyage for the discovery of the northwest passage to India. He asks whether the company will undertake it, or allow private men to do so, with a grant to them of the sole trade by that route for certain years if they discover the passage. After an adjournment a general court decided to undertake the venture, and to raise the money by a voluntary levy of five per cent. on the subscriptions of the first voyage, from such members as chose to embark on the venture.

A new subscription book was accordingly sent round to the brethren. In January, 1602, the court confirmed their proceedings by a "standing and unchangeable decree" for the expedition to discover "the northwest passage to the East Indies."

Arrangements then proceed for the selection, survey, and purchase of two pinnaces with a total crew of thirty men at an estimated cost of £3000. Captain Waymouth agreed to conduct the voyage on payment of £100 for his instruments, with a promise of £500 if he discovered the passage, but without any remuneration if he failed. A question next arises as to whether the expedition will not infringe the chartered privileges of the Muscovy or Russia Company. The Muscovy Company take a high stand, yet offer to admit into their brotherhood such members of the East India Company as contribute to Captain Waymouth's expedition. After a wrangle between the two bodies, the East India Company apply to the Privy Council, which directs the Muscovy Company either to agree to joint action with the East India adventurers or to bring their patent before the Council for a scrutiny of their claim. The Muscovy Company give way, and finally the East India Company, having fortified themselves by a legal opinion, draw up instructions for the voyage, having recorded each step of their proceedings in the Court Minutes of 1601 and 1602.

A mass of detail follows, appointments of officers to the vessels, warrants for pork, wages, "hides to make the mariners' cassocks, breeches, and gowns." The victualling is divided among three sub-committees, and formal articles of agreement between Captain Waymouth and the company fill several pages. He is to pass through the Fretum Davies to the northwest to the "Kingdoms of Cataya or China," and not to desist from his course "so long as he shall find those seas or any part thereof navigable." This indenture was made in April, 1602.

The object of the expedition was, by means of a shorter northern route, to avoid "the long and tedious course" round the Cape of Good Hope, and the "many kinds of dangers offered therein." It was also thought that a less export of treasure from the realm would be required in trading with the nations of north Asia. A journal of the voyage was to be kept and a day-book of barters with the natives. Observations or discoveries were to be faithfully disclosed by Waymouth on his return to the governor, deputy governor, and committee-men of the company, and kept secret from all else. By another agreement, "John Cartwright of London, Preacher," was appointed chaplain to the expedition at £3 a month, only half of which was to be paid him unless one of the ships returned home by way of China.

Armed with a letter from Queen Elizabeth to the Emperor of China and Cathay, the expedition went forth and returned unsuccessful. Its failure was ascribed to the faint-hearted exhortations of Preacher Cartwright, and the directors demanded back from him "the gowne and apparell" in which he was to have figured at the Chinese court. The company also proceeded against Captain Waymouth before the Privy Council, but being satisfied with his defence, agreed to employ him on another voyage. Into his further history I need not enter. The subscribers to the northwest expedition of 1602 lost their money, its separate business was wound up, and the company proceeded to form new groups of adventurers for voyages by way of the Cape.

I have dwelt on Waymouth's expedition for two reasons. It illustrates the relations of the company to a particular voyage from the inception to the close of the venture; and it stands apart from the regular series of Cape voyages, so that I shall not have to refer to it again in my consecutive narrative of the Indian trade. The discovery of the northwest passage continued to be a dream of the East India adventurers, as it continued to be a dream of some of the most gallant seamen whom England has produced down to our day. In 1602 the company resolved to make "a final proof whether there be any passage or not," by means of Waymouth and another captain. In 1606 it granted a license to John Knight to discover the passage on his own account – in vain. For years afterwards the project reappears, and in 1614 the company was again being urged to seek a northern passage to Asia, with the promise of aid from the Emperor of Japan.

The permanent machinery by which the company carried on its business consisted from the first of a governor, deputy governor, treasurer, and a board of twenty-four committee-men, elected annually in July.

The same men were frequently re-elected. They were assisted by a secretary and accountant, also subject to re-election, and a small staff of clerks. As long as the company's business consisted in sending out separate voyages, this permanent board of management (represented by the Court of Committees) was much stronger than any of the separate bodies of subscribers, and kept the conduct of the separate voyages in its hands. But before the middle of the century, as we shall see, the separate bodies of subscribers overpowered the central body of management. The board of twenty-four committee-men became rather shadowy. The governor, deputy governor, and treasurer only retained their authority by acting as leading members of the separate ventures, in addition to their functions as permanent officials of the company. They thus exercised a unifying influence in the midst of conflicting and overlapping interests. For example, in 1647, when the adventurers of the Second General Voyage elected the committees who were to manage it, they expressly provided that "at every meeting Mr. Governor, Mr. Deputy, or Mr. Treasurer should be one."

The central board, including the governor, deputy, treasurer, and twenty-four committee-men, submitted all important arrangements for approval to meetings or "General Courts" of the freemen of the company, and were sometimes, although very seldom, overruled by the voice "of the generality." The capital which they managed consisted of the subscriptions for the separate voyages. Each new group of adventurers usually took over (under the direction of the company) the factors and property of the preceding venture; and the company thus acted as a link between the new group and its predecessor. The confusion of interests which arose out of this system will hereafter appear.

In the earlier stages of its history, the company or central board of management not only invested the capital raised for each separate venture, and conducted its business, but also appointed its servants. It handed over the agents in the East from their original group of employers to succeeding groups. A permanent body of English factors and employees in India thus developed and gave rise to many questions, such as private trade, which the company strictly forbade from the outset, and licensed trade, by which it allowed its servants to take a share in the ventures of the separate voyages. In its attitude to its servants, the East India Company preserved the domestic responsibilities of the medieval master-craftsman to his apprentices and men under his roof. At each factory the staff lived In one house, ate at the same table, met together for daily prayers, and had to be in by a certain hour at night. The early records are full of pious maxims and instructions as to brotherly conduct, "no brabbles," cleanliness of person, respect to superior officers and "the preacher," the care of health, and penalties for blasphemy or breaches of family morals. Gaming and dicing are strictly forbidden; excessive drinking and banqueting are denounced.

A single quotation from a strictly business letter, full of trade details, will illustrate this domestic aspect of the company. "And because there is no means more prevalent to strengthen and confirm the ways of the godly in righteousness than the spirit of God which is the guide into all good motions," the company wrote in 1610, "and no aid more pregnant to support and uphold the sinner from falling into wickedness than the grace of God, we exhort you in the fear of God to be very careful to assemble together your whole family [i. e. all the employees] every morning and evening, and to join together in all humility with hearty prayer to Almighty God for his merciful protection."

"Settle such modest and sober government in your household that neither amongst themselves there be contentious quarrels or other occasions of strife." "Comport yourself both in your habit [apparel] and housekeeping in such comely and convenient manner as neither may disparage our business nor be accounted too excessive in expenses."

Such instructions entered into every detail of the common family life of the factory, or trade settlement. Unnecessary shooting of salutes when captains went on shore, and the undue discharge of cannon at the drinking of healths, were repressed. Nor without cause, as the Portuguese sometimes spent so much gunpowder in vain ceremonials as not to leave enough to work their guns. Instead of salutes, it was eventually ordained that the English might cheer. They were to take an example from the Dutch, "who are very careful, industrious, and diligent," and to "trust none of the Indians, for their bodies and soules be wholly Treason." The company always mingled business with piety, from the fitting out of ships at Deptford to evening prayers in the Spice Islands, or the relief of English prisoners at Lisbon – to whom it sent two hundred ducats with the admonition "to comfort yourselves in the Lord."

"For the better comfort and recreation of such of our factors as are residing in the Indies," runs another document, "we have sent the works of that worthy servant of Christ, Mr. William Perkins," together with Foxe's "Book of Martyrs," and, one is glad to hear, "also Mr. Hackluit's Voyages to recreate their spirits with variety of history." Even their coat of arms, for which they paid "the King of Heralds" twenty marks in 1601, bears witness to the Puritanism of the city merchant of that day. It was not the well-known shield of 1698, with its lions for supporters, a lion holding a crown above, and the stately device of Auspicio Regis et Senatus Angliae. The earlier and almost forgotten arms of the company displayed three ships in full sail, with a pious pun as motto, Deus Indicat, God points the way.

We are now in a position to understand the mechanism and the methods by which the first English East India Company was to make its bid for the Asiatic trade, as against the more powerful Dutch corporation, and the united forces of Portugal and Spain. To recapitulate, it was at once a company for regulating the English trade to the East, and also for conducting that trade by subscriptions raised from successive groups of adventurers, who were generally members of its own body, or were admitted to it as subscribers. In one respect it resembled the medieval trade guild now represented by the London City Companies and "Lloyd's"; in another respect it resembled the modern limited liability company. From the first there was a tendency to divided interests between the successive groups of subscribers who found the capital and the permanent company who administered it. The conflict of these divergent forces determined the internal history of the company from its first charter of Elizabeth 'in 1600 to its reconstitution by Charles II in 1661.

From 1600 to 1612 there was a period of so-called Separate Voyages, each of which was theoretically complete in itself, and was to be wound up on the return of the ships by a division of the profits. During this period the power of the central company was supreme over each separate group of subscribers – subject, however, to the yearly election of its executive officers by the general body of members. But the sys-tem proved defective, as, owing to the length of the passage to India and the slow process of winding up, the separate voyages overlapped each other. It thus came about that the agents of several voyages were trading in India at the same time, and bidding against each other for spices and Indian products. Disputes and acts of ensued. Thus a ship of one voyage would refuse to carry home goods lying at Bantam for transport because they belonged to another group of adventurers.

The second period, from 1612 to 1661, was marked by efforts to remedy this state of things. It is known as the period of Joint Stocks. Each subscription was raised not for a single voyage, but for several, or to carry on the trade during a certain number of years. The central company still managed the business of each successive Joint Stock, as it had managed the business of each Separate Voyage from 1600 to 1612. But as the Joint Stock group lasted over a longer period than the Separate Voyage, it tended to become stronger than the central company, and to take the management of its business into its own hands. The idea was still present, however, that each Joint Stock would be wound up after a time and its profits finally divided, as in the case of the Separate Voyages. But practically the Joint Stock ventures and "General Voyages" were found to overlap each other as the Separate Voyages had done, and a similar confusion resulted.

A third stage was reached in 1661, when long adversity had taught the central company and the Joint Stock groups alike that conflicting interests must be fatal to their existence in the East. The idea that the Joint Stock was in due time to be wound up gradually disappeared. After the .Restoration the practice of buying and selling shares became common. This indicates that the Joint Stock principle had passed the stage represented by the second period from 1612 to 1661, and that the system was approaching more closely to the Joint Stock companies of our own times.

Appendix – Allusions by Mohammedan Historians to Europeans in India

As an appendix to this volume, in which the history of the early struggle by Europeans to gain a foothold in India is recounted in such detail, it may not be out of place to present some allusions to these foreigners (Firingis) by Mohammedan writers contemporary with the events described. The selections have been made from various parts of Elliot's "History of India as told by its own Historians," and, although not exhaustive, they are nevertheless in a way representative of the native view and may perhaps interest the reader as much as they did me in collecting and editing them.

A.V.W.J.

The Fort of Surat erected by Akbar in Opposition to the Portuguese

Akbar's imperial annalist, Badauni, when describing the emperor's campaign in Surat, 1572 – 1573 A.D., records that the erection or rebuilding of the Fort of Surat was in direct defiance of European intrusion and in opposition to foreign influence upon the Mohammedans of the country. A similar account is given by Nizam-ad-din Ahmad, but that of Badauni is a trifle clearer and is therefore the one here presented.

[Elliot, vol. v,.] 'One day in the year 980 A.H. (1572 A.D.) Akbar, the king, went to look at the Fort of Surat, and gave orders to repair the portions that had been battered and destroyed. During his inspection he saw the large mortars, which had been despatched with a powerful fleet and army by Sultan Sulaiman, the Turkish emperor, to assist in capturing the harbours of Gujarat, and had been left on the seashore, covered with rust, because Sulaiman Aga, the admiral, had abandoned the enterprise through meeting with some obstacle.

There they remained, until Khudawand Khan, the vizir, had them carried into the fort of Surat, at the time it was building. The few which remained had been taken to Junagarh by the governor. The king inspected them, and gave orders that some of them, which were not wanted there, should be sent to Agra.

The reason assigned for Khudawand Khan's building the fort of Surat is that the Firingis used to oppress the Mussulmans in every kind of manner, devastating the country and tormenting God's servants. At the time of laying the foundations of the fort, they tried to throw every obstacle in the way, by firing cannon from their 'ships, but all without effect.

That expert engineer laid the foundations of one side within the sea; dug a deep ditch round the two sides which faced the land, and built the walls with stones and burnt bricks. The wall was thirty-five yards long. The breadth of the four walls was fifteen yards, and their height twenty yards, and the breadth of the ditch was twenty yards. All the stones, the joints, and interstices were fastened together with iron clamps and made firm with molten lead. The battlements and embrasures were lofty, and so beautiful that everyone was astonished at beholding them. On the bastions, which projected into the sea, was erected a gallery (ghurfa), which the Firingis, especially the Portuguese, profess to say is an invention of their own. When the Mussulmans began to erect this chaukandi (turret), the Firingis exerted every kind of opposition to obstruct it; and when they found they could not prevail by force, they offered large sums of money to prevent its being built; but Khudawand Khan, through the regard which he bore to his own religion, sternly refused, and plied the , . work till it was finished, in contemptuous defiance of the Christians.'

Europeans at Akbar's court

In his well-known work, Akbar Namah, Abu-l-Fazl, the learned historian of Akbar's court, refers several times to the European Christians, and one of the earliest of these references is in connection with the siege of Surat, already alluded to, in 1571–1573, the seventeenth year of the emperor's reign. The brief mention is as follows:

[Elliot, vol. v,.] While the siege of Surat was proceeding, a large party of Christians arrived from the port of Goa and were admitted to an audience with the emperor Akbar, although it is probable that they had come to assist the besieged and to get the fort into their own hands. But when they saw the strength of the imperial force and its power for carrying on the siege, they represented themselves to be ambassadors and besought the honour of an interview. They offered various articles of the country as presents. Akbar treated each of them with great condescension and con-versed with them about the affairs of Portugal and other European matters.'

There is a special allusion, four years later, in Abu-l-Fazl's chronicles, to European articles at Goa and to novelties imported from abroad.

[Elliot, vol. v,.] Haji Habib had been sent to the port of Goa, with a large sum of money and intelligent artizans, to examine and bring to the knowledge of the emperor Akbar the various productions of art and skill to be found in that town. He now returned to court, having with him a number of men clad in Christian garb, beating drums and playing European instruments. He presented fabrics which he had selected. The artizans who had gone there to acquire knowledge exhibited their skill and received applause. Musicians of that country played upon various instruments, especially upon the organ, and gave great delight to all who heard them.'

In his annals for the twenty-third year of Akbar's reign, 1579 A.D., the royal chronicler deems the arrival of a European and his wife an incident of sufficient note to mention directly after he has recorded a matter relating to the imperial tribute due from the district of Bengal.

[Elliot, vol. v,.] While the emperor Akbar was encamped at the river Biyah, letters arrived from Khan Jahan, accompanying the tribute from Bengal, and from Raja Mal Gosain, the zamindar of Kuch, who had renewed his allegiance to the imperial throne. The tribute of Bengal consisted of the choicest productions of Bengal, and of fifty-four elephants. Along with these came a European named Partab Bar, who was accompanied by Barsuba, his wife[3]. He was graciously received at court, and his sound sense and upright conduct won the favour and esteem of the emperor.'

In the same year, 1579 A.D., there is an extended account of a religious discussion held at Akbar's "Hall of Worship" by a Christian padre from Portugal. Abu-l-Fazl's description is much to the point.

One night the 'Ibadat-Khanah, or "Hall of Worship," was brightened by the presence of Padre Radalf[4], who for intelligence and wisdom was unrivalled among Christian doctors. Several carping and bigoted men attacked him, and this afforded an opportunity for a display of the calm judgment and justice of the assembly! These men brought forward the old received assertions, and did not attempt to arrive at truth by reasoning. Their statements were torn to pieces, and they were nearly put to shame; and then they began to attack the contradictions in the Gospel, but they could not prove their assertions.

With perfect calmness and earnest conviction of the truth, the Padre replied to their arguments, and then he went on to say, "If these men have such an opinion of our Book, and if they believe the Koran to be the true word of God, then let a furnace be lighted, and let me with the Gospel in my hand, and the Moslem priests with their holy book in their hands, walk into that testing-place of truth, and the right will be manifest." The black-hearted, mean-spirited disputants shrank from this proposal, and answered only with angry words.

This prejudice and violence greatly annoyed the impartial mind of the Emperor, and, with great discrimination and enlightenment, he said: "Man's outward profession and the mere letter of Mohammedanism, without a heartfelt conviction, can avail nothing. I have forced many Brahmans, by fear of my power, to adopt the religion of my ancestors; but now that my mind has been enlightened with the beams of truth, I have become convinced that the dark clouds of conceit and the mist of self-opinion have gathered round you, and that not a step can be made in advance without the torch of proof. That course only can be beneficial which we select with clear judgment. To repeat the words of the Creed, to perform circumcision, or to lie prostrate on the ground from dread of kingly power, can avail nothing in the sight of God:

"Obedience is not in prostration on the earth:

Practise sincerity, for righteousness is not borne upon the brow.'" ·

Of a somewhat similar character is a reference in the thirty-fifth year of Akbar's reign, 1591 A.D., to the coming of a friar to the court. The spelling of the priest's name in the Arabic characters of the original text seems to be "Farmaliun," but they may be read in several other ways.

[Elliot, vol. v,.] 'At this time [i.e. 1591 A.D.], Padre Farmaliun (?) arrived at the imperial court from Goa, and was received with much distinction. He was a man of much learning and eloquence. A few intelligent young men were placed under him for instruction, so that provision might be made for securing translations of Greek books and of extending knowledge. With him came a number of Europeans and Armenians, who brought silks of China and goods of other countries which were deemed worthy of his Majesty's inspection.'

The account given by Badauni of the Christian missionaries at Akbar's court has been mentioned in the two preceding volumes of the present series (iv. 41; v. 284), but is here repeated in full because of its interest in connection with the preceding statements.

[Elliot, vol. v,.] 'In 986 A.H. (1578 A.D.) the missionaries of Europe, who are termed Padres, and whose chief pontiff, called Papa (Pope), promulgates his interpretations for the use of the people and issues mandates that even kings dare not disobey, brought their Gospel to King Akbar's notice, advanced proof of the Trinity, affirmed the truth of the Christian faith, and spread abroad the knowledge of the religion of Jesus. The king ordered his son, Prince Murad, to learn a few lessons from the Gospel, and to treat it with all due respect, while Shaikh Abushl-Fazl was ordered to translate it. Instead of the prefatory Bismillah, the following ejaculation was enjoined: "0 thou whose name is merciful and bountiful." To this Shaikh Faizi added: "Praise be to God! there is no one like thee – thou art he!" The attributes of the abhorred Anti-Christ were ascribed to our holy Prophet by these lying impostors.'

Europeans Grant Passes for Ships to Mecca

The increasing number of Christians in India and the fact that they were in a position to exact and grant passes to Moslems who used their ships on the way to Mecca was curiously employed by some Mohammedans (not without scorn) as an argument against pilgrimages. Badauni holds such a view up to ridicule in describing a scene in Akbar's "Hall of Worship."

[Elliot, vol. v,.] 'One night during the year 983 A.H. (1575 A.D.), Khan Jahan mentioned that Makhdum-al-Mulk had expressed an opinion that in those days it was not a religious duty to go on a pilgrimage, and that it was even sinful to do so. When he was asked his reasons, he replied that there were only two routes to Mecca, one was by Irak, the other by Gujarat. On the former route a man must hear abusive language from the Kazilbashes (Persian Shiahs); by the latter he must, before he embarks at sea, suffer the indignity of entering into an engagement with the Firingis, which engagement was headed and stamped with portraits of the Virgin Mary and Jesus Christ (upon whom be peace!), and so is tinctured with idol worship. Therefore both ways should be prohibited.'

The fact that the Europeans did grant passes for ships to convey pilgrims to Mecca is recorded also by Nizam-ad-din Ahmad, in the Tabakat-i Akbari, in which Akbar's historian notes incidentally that a ship was detained at Surat for lack of the necessary papers.

[Elliot, vol. v,.] 'When the emperor reached Udaipur, a despatch arrived from the port of Surat, from Sultan Khwaja, the Mir Haji of the port, announcing that the ship was useless as no pass (kaul) had been obtained from the Europeans. Akbar directed a messenger to be sent to Kalij Khan in order to despatch him speedily to Surat, so as to secure the departure of the vessel. ... Kalij Khan was accordingly sent to Surat to despatch the ships. He went along with Kalyan Rai, a merchant, and having obtained the passes from the Europeans, he sent off the ships and quickly returned and waited upon his Majesty while he was in Malwa.'

Europeans under Jahangir's Reign

A number of references to the position of Europeans in India during the reign of the Great Moghul emperor Jahangir (1605–1628 A.D.) have been made in the fourth volume of the present series, especially in connection with Hawkins and Sir Thomas Roe. There are several references in Jahangir's own Memoirs to the Europeans, Portuguese and English, which are worth recording. The first relates to outrages committed by the Europeans at Goa upon native ships trading at Surat. Jahangir writes the following in an entry under the eighth year of his reign, 1022 A.H. (1613 A.D.):

[Elliot, vol. vi,.] 'News arrived that the Europeans in Goa, in defiance of their engagements, had plundered four ships engaged in the foreign trade of the port of Surat; and having made a great many Mohammedans prisoners, had at the same time taken possession of their money and goods. It gave me much displeasure. Mukarrab Khan, the governor of that harbour, was presented with a robe of honour, besides an elephant and a horse, and was commanded to put a stop to such outrages.'

A year later, in 1614, the ninth year of his reign, Jahangir records with satisfaction the fact that the Portuguese and English (Angriz) had come into conflict at Surat, with the result that the Portuguese were wholly discomfited. He writes:

[Elliot, vol. vi,.] Happy tidings came of the defeat of the Portuguese (Warzi), who had made every preparation for the capture of the port of Surat. An action took place between them and the English (Angrizan), who had sought refuge in that port. Most of their vessels were burnt by the English, and not being able to stand the contest, they took to flight and sent a message to Mukarrab Khan, the governor of the ports of Gujarat, suing for peace and representing that they had come with peaceful views, not to fight, and that the English had been the first to quarrel.'

Of less historic importance, but hardly less interesting, is the fact gravely recorded by Jahangir regarding the first European carriage in India, in 1616, the eleventh year of his reign. It was the year when Sir Thomas Roe came as English ambassador to the Moghul court. It is interesting to compare the ambassador's description of the occasion (reproduced on the next page) with the paragraph in Jahangir's own Memoirs, where he refers to the equipage from Europe.

'On the afternoon of the first of Zu-l-ka'da, corresponding with twenty-first of Aban [1025 A.H., November 10, 1616 A.D.], I departed in sound health from Ajmir in a European carriage drawn by four horses, and I ordered several nobles to make up carriages similar to it5 and to attend upon me with them. About sunset I reached my camp in the village Deo Rana, a distance of nearly two leagues6.'

Europeans at Hugli in Shah Jahan's Time, 1628–1659 A.D.

The contemporary account given by Khafi Khan of the European settlement at the Port of Hugli, near Calcutta, is interesting as illustrating in certain respects the native attitude toward the foreign settlers.

[Elliot, vol. vii,.] The Firingis had formed a commercial settlement at Hugli, about twenty leagues from Rajmahal in Bengal. In former times they had obtained the grant of a parcel of land for the stowing of their merchandise and for their abode. There they built a strong fort, with towers and walls, and furnished it with artillery. They also built a place of worship which they call "church" (kalisa). In course of time they overstepped the sufferance that they had obtained. They vexed the Mussulmans of the neighbourhood and harassed travellers, and were continually exerting themselves to strengthen their settlement.

Of all their odious practices the following was the worst: In the ports which they occupied on the seacoast, they offered no injury either to the property or person of any of the Mohammedans or Hindus who dwelt under their rule; but if one of these inhabitants died, leaving children of tender age, they took both the children and the property under their charge, and, whether these young children were by birth Mohammedans, or whether they were of the religion of the Brahmans,they made them Christians and slaves. In the ports of the Konkan in the Deccan, and on the seacoast, wherever they had forts and exercised authority, this was the custom of that insolent people. But notwithstanding the notoriety of this tyrannical practice, Mussulmans and Hindus of all tribes went into their settlements in pursuit of a livelihood and took up their abode there.

They allowed no religious mendicant to come into their bounds. When one found his way in unawares, if he was a Hindu, they subjected him to such tortures as made his escape with life very doubtful; and if he was a Mussulman, they imprisoned and tormented him for some days, and then set him at liberty. When travellers passed in and their baggage was examined for the custom duties, no leniency was shown if any tobacco was found, because there were regular licensed sellers of tobacco, and a traveller must not carry more than enough for his own use.

Unlike a Hindu temple, their place of worship was very conspicuous, for tapers of camphor were kept burning there in the daytime. In accordance with their vain tenets, they had set up figures of the Lord Jesus and Mary (on our Prophet, and on them be peace!), and other figures in wood, paint, and wax, with great gaudiness. But in the churches of the English, who are also

Christians, there are no figures set up as idols. The writer of these pages has frequently gone into that place and has conversed with their learned men, and here records what he has observed.

Reports of the unseemly practices of these people reached the emperor Shah Jahan, and when Kasim Khan was sent to Bengal as governor, he received secret orders to suppress them and to take their fortress. Kasim Khan accordingly proceeded to Hugli and laid siege to it. The detail of his skilful arrangements and strenuous exertions would be of great length; suffice it to say that, by the aid of boats, and by the advance of his forces both by land and water, he brought down the pride of those people and subdued their fortress after a siege of three months. Nearly fifty thousand peasants of that place came out and took refuge with Kasim Khan. Ten thousand persons, Firingis and natives, perished in the course of the siege. Fourteen hundred Firingis, and a number of persons who had been made Christians by force, were taken prisoners. Nearly ten thousand persons, innocent natives and captives of those people, were set free. More than a thousand Mussulmans of the imperial army fell in the course of the siege.'

A fuller description of the port and of the manner in which Shah Jahan drove out the "infidel Firingis," in 1632 A.D., is given by Abd-al-Hamid, of Lahore, in his Padshah Namah.

'Under the rule of the Bengalis, a party of Frank merchants who were residents of Sandip came trading to Satganw. One league above that place, they occupied some ground on the bank of the estuary, where they erected several houses in the Bengali style on the pretext that buildings were necessary for their transactions in buying and selling. In course of time, through the ignorance and negligence of the rulers of Bengal, these Europeans increased in number and erected large substantial buildings, which they fortified with cannons, muskets, and other implements of war.

In course of time, a considerable place thus grew up, which was known by the name of the Port of Hugli. On one side of it was the river and on the other three sides was a ditch filled from the river. European ships used to go up to the port and trade was established there, while the markets of Satganw declined and lost their prosperity. The villages and districts of Hugli were on both sides of the river and the Europeans got possession of them at a low rent, and converting some of the inhabitants to their own faith, sent them off afterwards in ships to Europe7. These practices were not confined to the lands they occupied, but they seized and carried off every one they could lay their hands upon along both sides of the river.

These proceedings had come under the notice of the emperor before his accession, and he resolved to put an end to them if ever he ascended the throne. After he became Sultan, therefore, he appointed Kaska Khan to the government of Bengal and impressed upon him the duty of overthrowing these mischievous people, ordering him, as soon as he had attended to the necessary duties of his extensive province, to set about the extermination of the pernicious intruders. Troops were to be sent both by water and land so that this difficult enterprise might be quickly and easily accomplished.

Kasim Khan immediately began his preparations and at the close of the cold season, in Sha'ban, 1040 A.H. (1630 A.D.), he sent his son Inayat-Allah with Allah Yar Khan, who was to be the real commander of the army, and several other nobles to effect the conquest of Hugli. He also sent Bahadur Kambu, an active and intelligent servant of his, with the force under his command, ostensibly to take possession of the exchequer lands at Makhsusabad, but really to join Allah Yar Khan at the proper time. For fear that the infidels would put their families on board ship as soon as they heard of the movements of the troops, and would thus escape from destruction to the disappointment of the warriors of Islam, it was given out that the forces were marching to attack Hijli.

It was accordingly arranged that Allah Yar Khan should halt at Bardwan, which lies in the direction of Hijli, until he should receive intelligence of Khwaja Sher and others, who had been ordered to proceed in boats from Sripur (Serampur) to cut off the retreat of the Europeans. It was planned that when the flotilla should arrive at Mohana, Allah Yar Khan was to march with all speed from Bardwan to Hugli and fall upon the infidels. Upon being informed that Khwaja Sher and his companions had arrived, Allah Yar Khan made a forced march from Bardwan, and in a night and day reached the village of Haldipur between Satganw and Hugli. At the same time he was joined by Bahadur Kambu, who arrived from Makhsusabad with five hundred horse and a large force of infantry. He then hastened to the place where Khwaja Sher had brought the boats, and he formed a bridge of boats in a narrow part of the river, between Hugli and the sea, so that ships could not get down to the sea, thus preventing the enemy from escaping.

On the second of Zu-l-hijja, 1041 A.H. (1631 A.D.), an attack was made on the Europeans by the boatmen on the river and by the forces on land. An inhabited place outside of the ditch was taken and plundered, and the occupants were slain. Detachments were then ordered to the villages and places on both sides of the river, so that all the Christians found there might be put to death. Having killed or captured all the infidels, the warriors carried off the families of their boatmen, all of whom were Bengalis, whereupon four thousand boatmen left the Europeans and joined the victorious army, thus greatly discouraging the Christians.

The royal army was engaged for three months and a half in the siege of this strong place. Sometimes the infidels fought and sometimes they made overtures of peace, protracting the time in hopes of succour from their countrymen. With base treachery they pretended to make proposals of peace and sent almost a hundred thousand rupees as tribute, while at the same time they ordered seven thousand musketeers who were in their service to open fire with their guns. So heavy was their fusillade that many of the trees of a grove in which a large force of the besiegers was posted were stripped of their branches and leaves.

At length the besiegers sent their pioneers to work upon the ditch just by the church, where it was not so broad and deep as elsewhere. There they dug channels and drew off the water, after which mines were driven on from the trenches, but two of these were discovered by the enemy and countermined. The centre mine was carried under an edifice which was loftier and stronger than all the other buildings, and in which a large number of Europeans were stationed. This was charged and tamped, and on the fourteenth of Rabi'-al-awwal, 1042 A.H. (1632 A.D.), the besiegers' forces were drawn up in front of this building to lure the enemy in that direction. When a large number were assembled, a heavy fire was opened and the mine was ignited. The building was blown up and many Europeans who had collected around it were sent flying into the air. The warriors of Islam then rushed to the assault, whereupon some of the infidels were drowned in the water8, but some thousands succeeded in making their way to the ships. At this juncture Khwaja Sher came up with the boats and killed many of the fugitives.

Since these European foes of the Faith of Islam were afraid lest one large ship, which had nearly two thousand men and women and much property on board, might fall into the hands of the Mohammedans, they fired the magazine and blew her up. Many others who were on board the ghrabs, or smaller vessels, set fire to them and thus met their deaths. Out of the sixty-four large dingas, fifty-seven ghrabs and two hundred jaliyas, only one ghrab and two jaliyas escaped in consequence of some fire from the burning ships that had fallen upon some boats laden with oil and burnt a way through the bridge of boats. Whoever escaped from the water and fire, became a prisoner. From the beginning of the siege to its conclusion, almost ten thousand of the enemy, men and women, old and young, were killed, being either blown up with powder, drowned in water, or burnt by fire; nearly one thousand brave warriors of the imperial army obtained the glory of martyrdom; 4400 Christians of both sexes were taken prisoners; and well-nigh ten thousand inhabitants of the neighbouring country who had been kept in confinement by these tyrants were set at liberty.'

Some ten years later, in 1633, the Emperor Shah Jahan again took active measures against the Christians, as we are told by Abd-al-Hamid, the Mohammedan annalist whose work has just been quoted.

[Elliot, vol. vii,.] 'On the eleventh of Muharram [in the year 1043 A.H., 1633 A.D.], Kasim Khan and Bahadur Kambu brought four hundred Christian prisoners, male and female, young and old, with the idols of their worship, to the presence of the Faith-defending Emperor [Shah Jahan]. He ordered that the principles of the Mohammedan religion should be explained to them, and that they should be called upon to adopt it. A few appreciated the honour offered to them and embraced the faith; these few experienced the kindness of the Emperor. But the majority in perversity and wilfulness rejected the proposal. These were distributed among the amirs, who were directed to keep these despicable wretches in rigorous confinement. When any one of them accepted the true faith, a report was to be made to the Emperor, so that provision might be made for him. Those who refused were to be kept in continual confinement. So it came to pass that many of them passed from prison to hell. Such of their idols as were likenesses of the prophets were thrown into the Jumna, the rest were broken to pieces.'

Customs of the Europeans at Hugli in Mohammad Shah's Time, 1719–1748 A.D.

A native writer of Kashmir, named Khwaja Abdal-Karim Khan, gives some account of the various European nations in India early in the eighteenth century, and comments on their manners and customs at Hugli in Bengal.

[Elliot, vol. viii,.] 'At this time [about 1743 A.D.], in consequence of the weakness of his Majesty Mohammad Shah, and the want of unanimity among his nobles, the armies of the Marathas of the south had spread themselves over Bengal, and Hugli fell into their hands. I had occasion to stop at the city of Firashdanga (Chandarnagar), which is inhabited by a tribe of Frenchmen. The city of Calcutta, which is on the other side of the water and is inhabited by a tribe of English who have settled there, is much more extensive and thickly populated than Firashdanga.

All the different tribes of Europeans have different names, such as the Fransis (French), Angriz (English), Walandiz (Hollanders), and Partagis (Portuguese). The delightful gardens which the Europeans make, with a number of trees great and small, all cut with large shears and kept in order, as in their own country, are exceedingly pleasing and refreshing They have so many gardens because a separate family, or one set of inhabitants, lives in a separate house.

There is no difference whatever to be observed in any of their manners and customs; indeed, they all live just as they do in their own country. They have churches, too, where they perform divine service in congregations, and everything else is managed in a similar way according to custom. Many tradesmen and professors of different arts have come from Europe and taken up their abode here, and get occupation in making things, carrying on their trade as they do in their own land. A great many of the Bengalis have become skilful and expert from being with them as apprentices.

As the Europeans excel in other arts and sciences, so also are they distinguished from the military point of view. This the Marathas know well; for although there is so much property and merchandise belonging to commercial and wealthy men of these parts in Firashdanga and Calcutta, and it would only be a journey of two leagues from Hugli to Firashdanga, and although the Europeans have no fort and are so few in number, while the Marathas are as numerous as ants or locusts, yet, in spite of all this, the Marathas see the unanimity and concord that exist among the Europeans, and do not attempt to approach them, much less to attack them. The Europeans fight with guns and muskets; but when the time for using the sword comes, they are at a disadvantage.'

European Christians Contend Against the Mohammedans in Malabar and the Deccan (1500 1600 A.D.)

In a native history of India written about the year 1800 A.D. by Nawab Muhabbat Khan (who is not to be confused with his contemporary and namesake, the second son of Hafiz Rahmat), there is an extensive account of the conflicts between the Mohammedans and the European Christians who had come into Malabar and the Deccan during the sixteenth century.

[Elliot, vol. viii,.] 'Let it not be hidden from the sun-resembling minds of those who understand the value of the gems of intelligence that, previous to the rise of Mohammedanism, the Jews and the Christians had intercourse, as merchants, with most of the ports of the Deccan, such as Palniar9 and others. Having become familiar with the people of that country, they established their residence in some of the cities, and built houses and gardens.

In this manner they sojourned for many years. When the great star of Mohammedanism appeared and the rays of that world-enlightening sun shone from the east to the west, the countries of Hindustan and the Deccan were also gradually benefited by the light of the Mohammedan law, and intercourse of the Mussulmans with that country began. Many of the kings and rulers of that country espoused the Mohammedan faith. The Rajas of the ports of Goa, Dabal, and Chand, and other places allowed all the Mussulmans who came there from the different parts of Arabia to settle on the seashore, and treated them with great honour and respect.

For this reason the Jews and. Christians burned with the fire of envy and malice. But when the countries of the Deccan and Gujarat came into the possession of the Kings of Delhi, and Islam was established in them, the Europeans put the seal of silence on their lips and never uttered a word of animosity or opposition, till at length, about the year 900 A.H. (1495 A.D.), when weakness and disorder found their way into the government of the Sultans of the Deccan, the Portuguese Christians received orders from their king to build their forts on the shore of the Indian Ocean.

In the year 904 A.H. (1499 A.D.) four ships of the same people arrived at the ports of Kandaria and Kalikot (Calicut), and having made themselves acquainted with the circumstances of the place, returned to their own country. Next year six vessels came and anchored at Kalikot. The Portuguese petitioned the chief of the place, who was called Samuri (Zamorin), to prohibit the Mohammedans from intercourse with Arabia, remarking that they would benefit him much more than the Mohammedans could. The Samuri, however, gave no heed to their prayers, but the Christians began to deal harshly with the Mohammedans in all their transactions.

At last the Samuri (Zamorin), being provoked, gave orders that the Christians should be slain and plundered. Seventy persons of rank were destroyed among the Christians, and those who remained embarked on the vessels and thus saved themselves. They landed near the city of Koji (Cochin), the chief of which was at hostility with the Samuri. They obtained his permission to build a fort, which they completed hurriedly in a very short time They demolished a mosque on the seashore and made a Christian church of it. This was the first fort which the Christians built in India.

With the same expedition they built a fort at Kanur (Cannanore), and to their entire satisfaction engaged in the trade of pepper and dry ginger, preventing others from engaging in the same traffic. On this account the Samuri raised an army, and having killed the son of the chief of Cochin, plundered the country and returned. The heirs of those who were slain again collected their forces, raised the standard of sovereignty, and restored the population of the country to its former state. By the advice of the Firingis they built ships of war, and the chief of Cannanore followed their example. This excited the anger of the Samuri, who lavished immense treasure upon an army raised for the purpose of attacking Cochin; but as the Firingis always gave their assistance to its chief, the Samuri twice returned unsuccessful. The chief of Cannanore was at last obliged to send his ambassadors to the kings of Egypt, Jedda, the Deccan, and Gujarat, complaining to them of the outrages of the Christians and imploring their aid. At the same time he also represented their disrespect toward Islam and thus excited the wrath as well as the zeal of those princes. The Sultan of Egypt, Mansur Ghori, sent one of his officers named Amir Husain with thirteen ships (ghrabs) full of fighting men and munitions of war toward the coasts of Hindustan. Sultan Mahmud of Gujarat also prepared several ships to oppose the Firingis, and despatched them from the ports of Diu, Surat, Goga, Dabal, and Chand. The Egyptian vessels touched first at Diu, and joining those of Gujarat, sailed toward Chand, where the Firingis had assembled. This force was augmented by forty vessels of the Samuri, and by some, from the port of Dabal.

When the junction of the fleet was effected, a fire-ship of the Firingis, without being observed, suddenly fell upon its rear, and the whole surface of the water was instantly in a blaze. Malik Ayaz, the chief of Diu, and Amir Husain prepared to oppose the enemy, but all to no avail. Several Egyptian ships were taken by the enemy, numerous Mohammedans drank the sweet water of martyrdom, and the Firingis returned victorious to their port.

It was during these days that Sultan Salim of Rum obtained a victory over the Ghori Sultans of Egypt, and thus their dynasty closed. The Samuri, who was the originator of all these disturbances, was disheartened, and the Firingis obtained complete power; so much so, that in the month of Ramazan, 915 A.H. (Dec., 1509 A.D.), they came into Kalikot, set the Jami' Masjid on fire, and swept the city with the broom of plunder. Next day, the men of Palniar collected in large numbers, and falling upon the Christians, killed five hundred men of rank, and many were drowned in the sea. Those who escaped the sword fled to the port of Kou-lam (Quilon). Having entered into friendly relations with the zamindar of that place, they erected a fortress for their protection about half a league from the city.

In the same year they took the fort of Goa, belonging to Yusuf Adil Shah, who retook it by stratagem; but after a short time, the Firingis, having bribed the governor of the place with large sums of gold, again became its masters, and they made the fort, which was exceedingly strong, the seat of their government. This made sorrow and grief prey upon the health of the Samuri, who expired in 921 A.H. (1515 A.D.). His brother, who succeeded him, rolled up the carpet of destruction and pursued the path of friendship with the Firingis. He gave them ground for a fort near the city of Kalikot, and took an agreement from them that he should be allowed to send four ships laden with pepper and dry ginger to the ports of Arabia. For some time the Firingis observed these terms; but when the fort was completed, they prohibited his trading in those articles, and began again to practise all kinds of tyranny and persecution upon the followers of Islam.

In like manner, the Jews of Kranghir (Cranganore), observing the weakness of the Samuri, advanced their foot beyond the proper limit, and made a great many Mohammedans drink the cup of martyrdom. The Samuri, repenting of his concessions, marched toward Cranganore and so entirely extirpated the Jews that not a trace of them was found in that land. After this, joined by all the Mussulmans of Palniar, he proceeded to Kalikot and laid siege to the fort of the Firingis, which he reduced with great difficulty. This increased the power and pride of the men of Palniar, who, according to the terms of the original agreement with the Firingis, began to send their ships full of pepper, dry ginger, and other products to the ports of Arabia.

In the year 938 A.H. (1531 A.D.) the Firingis founded a fort at Jaliat, six leagues from Kalikot, and prevented the sailing of the Palnadi vessels. About the same time, during the reign of Burhan Nizam Shah, the Christians built a fort at Rivadanda, near the port of Chaul (Kolaba, Bombay), and took up their residence there. In the reign of Sultan Bahadur Shah of Gujarat, 941 A.H. (1534 A.D.), they took possession of the ports of Swalh, Daman, and Diu, which belonged to the kings of Gujarat, and in the year 943 A.H. (1536 A.D.) they fully established themselves at Cranganore by force of arms.

At this time Sultan Salim of Rum determined to expel the Firingis from the ports of India and make himself master of them. With this view, in the year 944 A.H. (1537 A.D.), he despatched his minister, Sulaiman Badshah, in command of one hundred vessels, and he, having wrested the port of Aden from Shaikh Amr, son of Shaikh Daud, whom he put to death, sailed to the port of Diu and there made preparations for war. He was nearly victorious, but, for want of provisions and money, he had to return unsuccessful to Rum.

In the year 963 A.H. (1556 A.D.) the Tarsas (Christians) were in possession of the ports of Ormuz, Muscat, Sumatra, Malacca, Mangalore, Negapatam, Barcelore, Ceylon, and Bengal, to the very borders of China.

In all these places they built their forts. But Sultan Ali Hai captured the fort of Sumatra from them, and the chief of Ceylon also, having subdued the Firingis, expelled them from his dominions. The Samuri, chief of Kalikot, being much harassed, sent his ambassadors to Ali Adil Shah and Murtaza Nizam Shah, instigating them to wage a holy war against the Firingis and turn them out of their country.

In 979 A.H. (1570 A.D.) the Samuri besieged the fort of Jaliat, and Nizam Shah and Adil Shah besieged that of Rivadanda. The former, through his courage, was successful in capturing the fort; but the latter, on account of the infidelity of their servants, who were deceived by the temptations which the Firingis offered them, returned without fulfilling their object.

From this time the Christians became more audacious in their persecution of the Mohammedans, in so far that they stretched out their rapacious hands to plunder on their return from Jedda some ships of the Emperor Jalal-ad-din Mohammad Akbar, which had sailed to Mecca without their permission, and they treated the Mussulmans with great severity and contempt. They burnt down the port of Adilabad Farain, which belonged to Adil Shah, and entirely destroyed it. In the guise of merchants, they also came to Dabal, and wished, by cunning and deceitful means, to obtain possession of it; but its chief, Khwaja Ali-al-Malik, a merchant of Shiraz, being aware of their views, killed 150 of their men of rank and devoted himself to extinguishing the fire of mischief.'

The Mohammedan historian then devotes a couple of paragraphs to the complete establishment of the English power in India.

[Elliot, vol. viii,.] Be it known to men of curiosity that from the time when the ships of the Emperor Akbar were seized by the Christians, the sending of vessels to the ports of Arabia and Persia was entirely closed, not only in the Deccan and Bengal, but also in other provinces of Hindustan, because it was considered beneath the royal dignity to enter into treaties with the Firingis, and to send treaties without entering into any understanding was to throw lives and property into danger. The Emperor's nobles, however, such as Nawab Abd-ar-Rahim Khan Khan-khanan, and others, having entered into an agreement with them, used to send their own ships, and affairs continued in this course for some time.

When the Emperor Jahangir ascended the throne of Delhi, there existed great discord and animosity between the Christians of Portugal, France, etc. Thirsting after the blood of each other, they read together the same evil book of hatred and malice. Contrary to the manner in which they had been treated, the Emperor Jahangir granted the English a spot in Surat for the erection of a factory. This was the first settlement which the English made on the coasts of India. Before this, they also occasionally brought their cargoes to the ports of Hindustan, and having sold them there, returned to their native country. Afterwards, they also began to establish their factories at different places in the Deccan and Bengal, and in the time of Aurangzib Alamgir they founded the city of Calcutta.'

Founding of the City of Calcutta

The founding of the city of Calcutta by Mr. Job Charnock, chief of the Bengal council, is assigned to the year 1686, although the site was an old one and the Portuguese had anchored there as early as 1530 in their trade with Hugli town, The city owes its name Calcutta to Kali-Ghat "Ghat of the goddess Kali," a famous Hindu shrine on the banks of the Hugh and now situated on the outskirts of Calcutta. The Mohammedan author Nawab Muhabbat Khan, who has been already quoted, thus describes the founding of the city.

[Elliot, viii, 379–382.] 'Calcutta was formerly only a village, the revenue of which was assigned for the expenses of the temple of Kali Devi, which stands there. As in the Bengali language the words Karta and Kat mean the proprietor of that Kali, in course of time, by the elision of the i it began to be called Calcutta10.

I now proceed to an account of the foundation of the city, and how the Honourable Company's factory was maintained at Gholghat and Moghulpura, near Hugh. Suddenly, at about sunset, when the English officers were at their dinner, a violent bore arose in the river and fell with such force upon the shore that the factory was in danger of falling down. The officers ran out in great consternation and saved their lives. All the goods and property were destroyed by the water, and a few men and several animals lost their lives.

Mr. Chanak (Job Charnock), their chief, having purchased the Benarasi Bagh, or "Benares Garden," which belonged to the Company's agent at Gholghat, near the city, cut down the trees and founded a factory, the buildings of which were raised two and three stories high. When the compound was made and the rooms were ready to be roofed in, the nobles and chief men among the Sayyids and Moghuls, who were great merchants, went to Mir Nasir, the magistrate of Hugh, and declared that if the strangers were allowed to ascend their lofty houses, they, the Moghuls, would be greatly dishonoured, seeing that the persons of their women would be exposed to view. The magistrate sent a report of the matter to Nawab Ja'far Khan and directed the Moghuls and other principal inhabitants of the place to accompany it.

They all complained before the Nawab, who issued orders to the magistrate to the effect that not another brick or timber should be allowed to be raised. That official, immediately on receipt of the order, prohibited all the masons and carpenters from carrying on the work, and ordered that no one should go to the factory. Thus the work remained unfinished.

Mr. Chanak, with great indignation, prepared to fight; but as he had a very small force, and as only one vessel was present at the time, while the Moghuls, who were joined by a powerful magistrate (whose name was Abd-al-Ghani), had assembled in great number, he saw no advantage in taking any hostile measure against them, and was obliged to weigh anchor. He had a burning-glass in his ship, with which, by concentrating the sun's rays, he burnt the river face of the city as far as Chandarnagar.

With a view to avenge this injury, the magistrate wrote to the police station at Makhua with orders to stop the vessel. The head constable accordingly, in. order to prevent the passage of the vessel, prepared an iron chain, each link of which was ten stirs in weight, and having made it in length equal to the breadth of the river, kept it ready and fastened it to the wall of the fort. The chain being extended across the river, the vessel was thus intercepted; but Mr. Chanak cut through the chain with a European sword, and went on his way. He took his vessel out to sea and proceeded toward the Deccan.

In those days the Emperor Aurangzib was in that part of the kingdom, straitened by his enemy for provisions, and his camp was reduced to starvation. Thereupon the chief of the factory in the Carnatic sent vessels laden with grain, showing great consideration for the throne, and proved of great service. The Emperor was much pleased with the English people and desired to know the Honourable Company's wishes. The English chief requested him to grant a sanad (warrant) and farman (order), giving permission to establish factories in all parts of the kingdom, and particularly in Bengal. The request was granted, and the royal orders exempting the Honourable Company's ships from custom duties, fixing a sum of three thousand rupees as a present to be given to the bakhshi of the port, and giving permission for the establishment of factories, were issued.

Mr. Chanak returned with the royal farmans from the Deccan to Bengal, and sent his agents with the gift and some presents to Ja'far Khan, and obtained permission to erect a factory in Calcutta. Mr. Chanak accordingly erected a new factory at the place where he anchored after returning from the Deccan, which is known by the name of Chanak. He founded the city and populated it, and gave a stimulus to the trade of Bengal. That factory is well known to this day by the name of the Old Fort.

Calcutta is a large city, situated on the banks of the Bhagirati. It is a large port and the great mart of the trade of the Honourable Company and their dependents. Small vessels called salap (sloops?) every year trade with this port from China, Europe, and other countries, and almost at all times some are at anchor there.

In these days this city is the residence of the chief English officers, and the city and its dependencies are considered their property. The buildings are built entirely of masonry stories high. The lower apartments are not fit to be inhabited. The buildings are like those of Europe, airy, spacious, and commodious, and are all constructed of brick. Besides the English merchants, the Bengalis, Armenians, and other inhabitants are also rich merchants. The water of the wells in the city is not drinkable on account of its brackish quality. If any person plastered with lime or mud. The land, on account of its vicinity to the sea, is very brackish and damp, and hence the houses are raised two or three drinks it, he is sure to suffer. In the hot and rainy seasons it becomes peculiarly bitter and saline, and consequently drinking water is procured from tanks.

The sea is forty leagues distant from the city, and the ebb and flow of the tide occur every day and every night. At full moon the bore rushes in for three days with unusual violence. It presents a curious and wonderful scene; it throws some boats on the shore, and breaks others to pieces; those which are not near the shore receive no injury from it, and therefore no boat, large or small, is left there unanchored. In the same manner, toward the end of the lunar month, the water rolls in with great violence for three days and nights. These high floods are called homan in the Bengali language, and that which takes place daily is termed jowarbhata.

A mud fort toward the south, outside the city, constructed after the English model, is very marvellous. Its praise is beyond all expression; it is well worth seeing. From the outside, the wall that encircles it appears low in every direction, just like the embankment of a tank; but from the inside it appears high. Very large and lofty buildings are erected within its enclosure, and much skill was shown in the entire construction of this fort. There are many other wonderful and excellent works in this city. As regards the beauty of the buildings and various novelties, there is no city like this in the whole of Hindustan, except Shah-Jahanabad, or New Delhi, with which nothing can be compared. The only defects of Calcutta are that the air is very insalubrious, the water brackish, and the soil damp, to such a degree that the floors of the houses are always damp from the excessive moisture, even though they are made of bricks and lime; and the walls likewise are wet to the height of two or three cubits. For four months in the winter the climate is not so unhealthy; but for eight months during the summer and rainy seasons it is very injurious.'

European Settlements at Chandarnagar and Elsewhere

Nawab Muhabbat Khan concludes his account of Calcutta with a panegyric of some thirty lines in verse, which is here omitted, but his next paragraph is given in full because it treats of the French settlement at Chandarnagar in Bengal, not far from Calcutta, and describes the settlements made at other places by the English, the Dutch, and the Danes.

[Elliot, vol. viii,.] 'Chandarnagar, otherwise called Firashdanga, is twelve leagues from Calcutta, and there is a factory in it belonging to the French Christians. It is a small town on the banks of the Bhagirati. An officer of the King of France remains there to govern the town and manage the commercial affairs of the place. The English have no concern with it. In the same manner, Chochra (Chinsurah) is in possession of the tribe of Walandiz (Hollanders). This place is a little to the south of the port of Hugli and is one league to the north of Firashdanga. In like manner, Seorampur (Serampur), which is also situated on the same stream, and opposite Chanak, has a factory of the tribe of Danamar (Denmark), by which name the station itself is sometimes called. In these places no other rule prevails than that of the nation which owns the factories.'